Praise from Readers

"This is one of the few 'how-to' books that really delivers on its promise. After just a week and a half and only halfway through the book, I had my first empty inbox experience, the dream of any email-enslaved professional. The book contains essential tips and tricks but also goes into the mindset and conceptions we all have, and that prevent us from being more efficient and more effective. We take driving lessons before we can take a car on the road. In the same way, you should read this book before you start using email."

* * *

"I love this book from Joost Wouters - so practical and so full of tips to get in control of email. Let's be honest, managing emails is a challenge, and Joost's strategies are just what I need. Highly recommend to anyone - senior executive, CEO, entrepreneur or just starting out on your career."

* * *

"This book has been excellent. I applied the methods that were taught in it and they were clear and very easy to follow. They have transformed my relationship with my inbox!"

* * *

"Like it or not, we all have to deal with email every day in our jobs or personal life. The bad news is that no one taught us to use it, and it usually ends up being a bottomless bucket. The good news is that Joost teaches you a simple step-by-step method to gain control of your inbox easily."

* * *

"I love Joost's powerful approach to inbox handling and I think you'll love it too."

* * *

"Thank you for teaching me how to liberate myself from my overloaded inbox! It's almost like when I gave up smoking - I've managed to kick a bad habit and I feel happier as I am no longer a prisoner to the addiction."

"I started to read this book on my flight back home, and after a few pages I was sorry not to have my laptop with me. Let me give you a small tip: read it with your Outlook open and start to implement the tips as you go through the book. It took me three days to get my inbox to zero emails, and more importantly I have kept it like this since then. Fantastic! A clear method to boost your productivity and to get more important things done."

* * *

"Ever since I started applying the rules from this book, I have been able to maintain my inbox as I would like."

* * *

"Not only does Wouters give you a workable system that helps you eliminate future emails from clogging your inbox, but he also tackles the most important issue which is how we think about the tool of email. Through changing your mindset and implementing solid tools, Wouters has found the formula to help busy professionals gain back potentially hours within their week. A truly great book and program!"

* * *

"What previously was an overloaded inbox is now literally a zero inbox on a daily basis. I'm so happy!"

* * *

"Since I emptied my inbox, it has been so easy to maintain. Now it only takes a couple of minutes, rather than an hour, to clean up my inbox, which allows me to concentrate on what I really should be doing - my job."

* * *

"FINALLY! A system for managing email that actually WORKS!"

* * *

"This book means a lot to me. I recommend this book to immediately target email habits without having to learn complicated routines."

* * *

THE
15-MINUTE
INBOX

Control Email. Create Time.
Lead Your Business.

Joost Wouters

Heartbeat Publishing

Published by Heartbeat Publishing
112 Senecalaan, 's-Hertogenbosch, The Netherlands

Author photograph by Muriel Janssen (@muur)
Edited by Lucy Goodchild (@LucyGoodchild)

First printing: March 2013
10 9 8 7 6 5 4 3 2

ISBN: 978-1483929736

www.15MinuteInbox.com

Also available as eBook and Audiobook

Dedicated to Frieda, Ruben, Jonas & Ginger.
My most important reasons to not spend all my time
in my inbox.

Contents

Introduction

You've Got Mail, Probably More Than Enough 1

Chapter One

Your Inbox as a Firm Foundation 3

Chapter Two

Reactive Fire fighter or Proactive Business Builder? 11

Chapter Three

The Most Precious Asset: Your Attention 22

Chapter Four

The M.A.I.L. System: Four Steps to Master Your Inbox 32

Step 1: M is for Mirrors and Mindsets

Chapter Five

The Email Culture You are Part of 42

Chapter Six

Your Email Behavior 55

Chapter Seven

It's All About Your Mindset 66

Step 2: A is for Actions and Automation

Chapter Eight

Tame the Flow of Incoming Email 77

Chapter Nine

Treat All and Touch Once: The 4+1 Action Ds 90

Chapter Ten

Speed Up Your Email Replying and Reading 99

Chapter Eleven

Deal With Your Backlog 111

Chapter Twelve

Create a Crystal Clear Archiving Architecture 116

Step 3: I as for Implementation and Integration

Chapter Thirteen

Create New Email Habits 125

Chapter Fourteen

Fall Seven Times, Stand Up Eight 137

Chapter Fifteen

When Email Goes Wrong 148

Step 4: L is for Leverage and Liberation

Chapter Sixteen

Leverage Email Awareness 160

Chapter Seventeen

Liberation: Where Is Your Plane Going? 169

Chapter Eighteen

Get Out of Your Inbox, Step Into Your Business 188

Epilogue

End of Message [EOM] 204

INTRODUCTION

You've Got Mail, Probably More Than Enough

"Information overload is a symptom of our desire to not focus on what's important. It is a choice." – Brian Solis

Email

Years ago, it was almost considered an event when you received one. Nowadays, however, it has become one of the biggest obstacles of productivity.

Email.

We love it and we hate it. It's a fantastic communication tool if you use it correctly, but a big energy drainer if your inbox is overloaded with it.

When did answering emails become part of your job? It was never meant to be part of it! And yet it always has been. Albeit in different shapes and sizes, exchanging information is, has been, and always will be one of the core activities of any business at any time. You just haven't had the opportunity to master this specific type of information exchange, especially not now that emails enter your inbox at the rate of 200 per day.

It's not so much about the emails, but more about how you deal with this type of communication. If you are like most of us, there is a huge step to be made in the way that you deal (or don't deal) with your emails.

This book is about taking control of your emails. It is about moving from the back seat to the driver's seat, becoming the master of your emails and learning how to spend no more than 15 minutes per day on managing your inbox. It is about becoming a proactive business builder instead of a reactive firefighter. It was written to help you understand why you can't resist checking your email all the time, and to help you experience a change in your email behavior and implement new email habits.

You will also create a crystal clear understanding of what you really want to do, where you can really make a difference, and where your attention is really appreciated. For most of the people most of the time, this is not their inbox.

You can do it. You can control your inbox and manage it in 15 minutes per day. You can create additional time by cutting out the waste of non-supportive email behavior. And you can learn how to spend it on activities that really matter.

I have done it, many others have done it, and you can do it too. You will learn to be in control of your inbox and figure out which of the messages that stream towards you day after day are worthy of every single minute that you invest in them... and which are not.

Remember: it is your time and your attention. It's your life. You can make this change. (Unless you enjoy fighting fires a lot.)

Welcome to *The 15-Minute Inbox*.

CHAPTER ONE

Your Inbox as a Firm Foundation

"A successful person is one who can lay a firm foundation with the bricks that others throw at him or her." – David Brinkley

Business A.M. (After Mail)

Email is great. Let there be no doubt about it. Email makes many things possible; from communication at a distance, to sending information at times when the recipient is busy or sleeping. Email made it possible for my family to move our office and our lives to the Mediterranean coast in Spain. When I realized I was communicating with my clients mainly via phone and email, the decision to move to a place with a higher quality of life – including more hours of sun – was a quick one.

Email has a down side, as well. Over the last few years the number of emails that an average manager receives per day has grown dramatically. We use email for many purposes; to send information, to invite people to a meeting, to fire people, or to fight with people. We also use it to agree or disagree with a statement, to suggest a new idea, or to avoid direct personal confrontation.

Email has changed the daily activity of today's managers. When

I work with my clients, I see more and more managers running their teams and business from behind their screens. Now, I'm not saying this is good or bad, but I have noticed that a lot of these managers are complaining about the constant flow of incoming emails, and the lack of time they have to deal with all of them properly. Let alone get on with their real business.

Managers try to stay on top of their email by adding additional hours to their already long, busy days; early in the morning when the office is still empty and quiet, or late in the evening at home with their family members around. They start to adopt the belief that email overload is something we have to live with. We tend to think that there is nothing we can do to put an end to it.

I will share and explain a concept that will make it possible for you to be in control of your email. You will learn to create time by eliminating the hours wasted on inefficient email behavior, and to use it instead on activities where you can really make a difference. This could be in your business, or in any other area of your life.

Business B.M. (Before Mail)

Before email played such a big role in our lives as managers, we had to deal with paper. When I started working at Procter & Gamble in 1995, I was dealing with a physical flow of documents coming in and going out. We did create our documents on computers, using Microsoft Word or Word Perfect, but they were printed and then distributed via the internal mail. Invitations, CVs, price lists, presentations, meeting minutes and reports all entered my inbox. I dealt with them, and I trashed them or filed them as needed.

Sometimes I wasn't successful in filing and keeping the information flowing. This had an immediate effect on my desk: it would grow like a wild garden. If I didn't take action and clean it up, my manager would pass by and suggest that I did. It was physically obvious if someone couldn't deal with information overload, and I'm sure that peer pressure helped a lot of us keep our desks clean.

With the increase of sending information via email, most of the paper has transformed into bits and bytes. However, the content of the information hasn't changed. I still receive invitations, CVs, price lists, presentations, meeting minutes and reports. And they still all reach me via my inbox, albeit a virtual one.

But then something strange happens. I don't deal with them all straight away, and I don't trash or file them all either. The amount of information I receive has grown tremendously, but my desk remains empty. And although my manager isn't walking past my desk suggesting I clean up, it feels like I am out of control. If I was to print all the emails in my inbox, with all their attachments and all their links, and put them on my desk, it wouldn't be a wild garden; it would be a jungle.

Even if it's not physically apparent, our inbox forms a big part of our desk. You don't want to work between piles of paper, and the same goes for stacks of electronic messages; you need to apply the same habits you used in Business B.M. to the virtual world of email.

An empty inbox creates clarity

Having an empty inbox isn't difficult at all. It requires some new habits and a bit of discipline. And the good news is that the moment you've experienced the benefits of an empty inbox, you will find the motivation to keep up the discipline.

It's not about following a strict and rigid email diet, or a Spartan inbox boot camp. It's not about saying goodbye to all the nice things that email brings – like the occasional joke or the great offer to fly to Amsterdam – by focusing only on boring and efficient email habits. It's about having a clear idea of where you add value, where you are appreciated and what you want to do. This almost certainly does not revolve around your inbox.

An empty inbox helps you stay on top of your business. It makes you more productive, by not having to check your email constantly, enabling you to work on your real priorities. An empty inbox creates clarity about what is and isn't important and it helps you avoid making mistakes or losing information. It keeps you in control and it makes you more responsive, and these are things people will notice.

What is your inbox about right now?

What's in your inbox right now? Do you have emails or do you have none? Do you know exactly what emails are there? More importantly, why are they still there? Are they there as a to-do list or for future reference? For your info? For follow-up? Or are they marked 'I really need to answer this when I have time'?

If you are anything like me, your inbox might contain a mixture of: information from previous projects, emails from peers, meeting minutes, an interesting offer for cheap flights, project specifications, newsletters with good tips on marketing (that I really should read), some jokes, some thought-provoking messages, some interesting LinkedIn connections that I should contact one day, some tasks I did in the past, an occasional spam message that made it through the filter, some references, some undeleted FYI mails from management, a couple of invoices I still need to pay… all unsorted, outdated, and probably useless.

Now if you look at your inbox right now, what story does it tell?

What kind of emails do you see? Personal, business, spam, newsletters, relevant, irrelevant? Or a mix of everything? And if you look at the time span between the oldest email in your inbox and today, is it days, weeks, months or years?

Make your answers factual. Don't feel bad about them. Face the reality. The only valid question at this point is: do you want to keep it this way?

Receive only what is relevant

In the ideal world, your inbox would only contain emails that are relevant to you. That includes answers to questions you have sent out, and information that you really need to progress with your top priorities.

Unfortunately, this is not the reality. I once read something saying that your inbox is a place where other people can too easily store their own agendas. This is exactly what happens. Your inbox is stuffed with other people's priorities, not yours. We think we are doing our jobs, but in fact we are constantly distracting ourselves from doing our jobs by granting time and attention to other people's agendas.

This is probably the most important insight you need in order to realize a life with less email stress. You first need to dedicate time to the things that are important to you, and to do the things you're responsible for in your own job. Then, if there is time left, you can focus your attention on other things and other people. It's like following the safety instructions in an airplane: first you put on your own oxygen mask, and then you help other passengers. These instructions are there for a reason! If you don't have your mask on, you can't help other people anymore: you're out of air.

There is one important requirement for successfully applying this approach. You need to be very clear about your job.

Are you clear about your job?

What are the most important objectives you need to achieve in your job?

How do you know you are doing a good job?

What are the KPIs on which your manager is measuring your performance?

What is the evidence you agreed in your personal development plan that will prove you did a good job?

What are the three things you want to accomplish today, no matter what?

If you could only spend time on one project, which one would it be?

What is the project that you have been postponing for weeks, that has a big risk of backfiring if you don't tackle it?

These are just a few questions to help you create clarity about your job. I strongly suggest you take a piece of paper and write down your answers. I would bet that, unless you're working in a Customer Service department, answering emails is not an answer to any of the questions.

So, if answering emails is not part of your job description, but is part of your daily reality, you need to get into gear. You are responsible for managing this distraction in your life so it doesn't interfere with your priorities.

In the next section you will explore how you can restore email and your inbox to what they are supposed to be: a communication tool to help you do things faster and more easily.

The M.A.I.L. System™

To support you on this journey, I have created the M.A.I.L. System. A simple, yet powerful process to help you stop wasting time and get things done - the things that really need to be done.

M – Mirrors and Mindsets

A – Actions and Automation

I – Implementation and Integration

L – Leverage and Liberation

If you search the internet, you will find a lot of good, practical advice on how to manage your email, deal with your inbox and get important things done. The challenge, however, is to implement this advice to affect your daily life.

To effectively change any habit, you need to look into the underlying beliefs. You also need to have a clear picture of what you want to achieve. This is something I have noticed while working with the management teams of many multinational companies over a decade of consultancy.

Each step of the M.A.I.L. system will introduce an important element needed to create a situation where you are in control of your inbox, not the other way around.

You will look at the mindsets and habits that you need to change to get your inbox under control in 15 minutes or less, each and every time you decide to spend time working on it. You will find ways to automate a big chunk of your email management, and you'll master all the actions you can take on each email. You will set up a structure that will help you implement the new behavior and make it part of your daily activities. And, most importantly, you will have a clear plan of what projects and activities you want to work on with all the additional time you have created.

You'll learn more about the M.A.I.L. system in Chapter Four.

CHAPTER TWO

Reactive Fire Fighter or Proactive Business Builder?

"There's never enough time to do all the nothing you want."
– Bill Watterson (Calvin and Hobbes)

Show me your inbox and I can tell you who you are

During my work as a consultant I have seen many inboxes, of different managers, at different companies, in different countries, and on all organizational levels. I once said to a manager that if she showed me her inbox I could tell her what kind of manager she was. She didn't believe me, so she challenged me to try. When I went through her inbox I noticed several things.

First of all, her inbox contained a lot of emails with requests for things that weren't under her responsibility. Because of this, I could tell she was either a very nice person who found it difficult to say no, or that she lacked clarity about what her real job and job responsibilities were and how she could best contribute to the organization. Secondly, her filing system was arranged in a very detailed way, with about 300 folders in trees of four to five layers deep, many folders containing only one email. This

11

told me that she found it difficult to make decisions. It also suggested that she probably wasn't proactively looking for ways to prioritize her day, but rather reactively waiting for what her inbox would tell her to do.

That's a lot of information from just looking at an inbox. And I wasn't far off with my conclusions.

So what is your inbox telling you? Are you in control of your day, or are you being controlled by the emails you receive? Are you empowering your team members, or do you micro-manage them by asking to be copied on everything? Are people around you clear about the things they should and shouldn't contact you for?

My email story

I used to spend a lot of time working in my inbox. When I arrived at work, the first thing I did was open my inbox; I was inevitably welcomed by a whole bunch of emails from previous weeks, plus plenty of new ones that had arrived the night before. So I would open one, skip one, delete one and take action on one, and before I knew it, it was an hour later and I was drawn further into the worlds of other people. I was always busy with actions that other people wanted me to take, and with information that was far from relevant for me at that moment.

I felt like a reactive fire fighter, rather than the proactive business builder that I wanted to be.

On top of that, my inbox was becoming a burden on my emotional well-being. I felt stressed that the work in my inbox was never done, my inbox was never empty, and I was overwhelmed by the vast number of emails that arrived every day. I felt out of control and I didn't know where to start with a to-do list as big as my inbox.

I was far from being productive. Every time I was working on something really important, the arrival of one new email in my inbox was enough to distract me, making me check if it was something even more important. And my team members weren't receiving answers to their questions in a timely manner, sometimes having to wait two or three days for something that they really needed to advance their jobs.

When I closed my laptop at night to go home, there was always this niggling feeling in the back of my mind that I had forgotten an important email. Before I fell asleep I was scrolling, be it subconsciously, through the inbox in my mind.

The solution

This continued until one day, some years ago, when I was coaching a client who was suffering from the same challenge (perhaps even worse). As a Director for Internal and External Communications, he was involved in heavy email traffic. In order to deal with his huge inbox, he was adding hours to his already long and fully packed days. At night, when he was at home with his wife and two daughters, he would spend a couple of hours dealing with all his emails. It was not the ideal situation.

When he asked me for a solution, we decided to tackle this problem once and for all. So I started studying. For months I surfed the internet, downloaded all the books available on the topic, read every blog and article written about email and managing email overload, and included the materials on productivity improvement I was already using in our own programs.

Based on all these ingredients I developed a complete concept to control email, create time and spend it on activities that really matter instead. But before I could help my client apply the concept, I had to see if it worked. So I followed my own advice. I did all the exercises I had developed, took the steps and undertook the practices. After three weeks I was clean! I didn't spend more than 15 minutes a day managing my inbox, I had an empty inbox at least once every day, the flow of incoming email had decreased dramatically and I was on top of my agenda and priorities.

I remember the feeling being fantastic, and you can imagine how proud I felt. When I went through the program with my client he had exactly the same results, including feeling proud. A great result!

The consequence of continuous connectivity

Of course, the internet and email are great. Things are possible now that were hard to imagine just a few years ago. I would be the last person to contradict this; the fact is that it is only possible to run our business out of Spain because of email and internet.

With smart phones and tablets, you can send and receive whatever you want to and from whoever you want, 24 hours a day, 7 days a week, 365 days a year. So we do.

However, this 24/7/365 connectivity has another side to it. We never actually learned how to deal with such an enormous amount of information. There is no subject at school or university that deals with prioritizing information, that teaches us which tools to use for which type of communication, or that shows us how to answer an email that has been upsetting us for two hours (here's a clue: you don't answer it).

What about the emotional effect of email? The fact that you can check your email at every moment of the day doesn't necessarily mean you should. Almost 25% of Americans[1] check their email just before going to sleep. Happy dreaming (or, rather, happy sex life).

The costs are enormous. Wasting just 60 minutes a day on the inefficiencies of email, such as reading long messages with an unclear action for you at the bottom, or deciphering an FYI mail only to find out that there is no added value for you, or simply deciding if you can delete a message, equals 25 lost days every year (given a 200-day, ten-hour working schedule). 25 days.

And 60 minutes a day is far below average. A recent PEW Internet Study[2] calculated that the average knowledge worker spends half their day working in their inbox, and that the annual costs for email inefficiencies is between 5,000 and 10,000 Euros per employee.

This means that a company with 500 employees loses between 2,500,000 and 5,000,000 Euros per year on email inefficiencies!

What is email overload costing you?

Let's have a look at your situation. How much time, on average, do you lose each day due to email and information overload? Be sure to include time you spend on:

- Dealing with being Cc'd or Bcc'd on a dozen messages and trying to figure out why
- Using email when voice or in-person would be faster
- Sending or receiving messages sent for 'butt-covering' reasons
- Decoding ambiguous, incomplete, or vague emails from someone in power
- Scanning and reading emails that turn out to be irrelevant
- 'Multi-tasking' because each email shoves you into a different train of thought

- Just calming down and re-centering from the anxiety of having a huge inbox backlog

---

Average time wasted on the above per day: _____ *minutes (A)*

Your annual salary: _____ *Euros/dollars/... (B)*

Working days per year: _____ *days (C)*

Working hours per day: _____ *hours (D)*

Total working days wasted per year:

(A * C) / (D * 60)

Total value of yearly wasted time:

(A * B) / (D * 60)

So, if you spend on average 60 minutes per day on all the inefficiencies of email (which is a low estimate), and you work 220 days per year for about 10 hours per day, with an annual salary of 100,000 Euros, you waste around 22 working days every year, which represents a value of 10,000 Euros.

Even if you're not so concerned about the wasted value, for me the loss of time is always staggering. What else could you do with 22 days?

No excuse

Nowadays, we accept the myth that email overload is part of our jobs and that we have to live with it. That it's a struggle and that there is no sustainable solution other than doing our best to keep it under control. And that the only thing we can do is to complain about it.

But that's a mistake.

There is no excuse for you not to master your inbox. There is no excuse for you not to know how to deal with all your emails. Being in control of your inbox and information flow is a management skill, just like knowing how to use Word, Excel or PowerPoint. In today's business world you cannot walk away from it. (Well, of course you can, but at what price?)

The higher your position in an organization, or the more influence you have on a group of people, the more important it becomes to master your inbox. People copy their leaders' behavior. Especially in times of stress. If you constantly send urgent emails, you distract your people from what they're doing. If you require a Cc on every email conversation that passes by, you train people not to make decisions themselves. And if you send emails with people in Bcc, you stimulate a political environment of distrust and suspicion.

Facing the challenge is not difficult

So, if you want an organization that is communicating in a constructive and proactive way, using email for what it is designed for (as a carrier for exchanging information, not as a replacement for personal communication), and at the same time to save yourself a huge amount of time on email inefficiencies, you must now face this challenge. And if you are not (yet) in a leadership role, saving time should be enough reason alone.

Facing this challenge is not complicated. It might not always be easy, but the way to create a situation where you control your email, and free up additional time you can spend on things that only you can do best, is simple. It requires discipline, commitment and a handful of new habits. That's all.

In my experience – based on my own journey and the work I've done with hundreds of others – it takes about two or three weeks to see huge results. And I mean huge. I mean spending just 15 minutes a day managing your email and having an empty inbox each time you've processed it (or at least once a day). Just a few weeks and you're in control.

By reducing the flow of incoming email, fine-tuning supportive email habits, training people around you on how best to deal with email, and improving the clarity of your own communication, you will notice improvements. Once you have implemented and integrated the basic habits, it becomes almost automatic. The approach will help you control the time you spend in your inbox rather than spending on your business, which, as I found out, makes a huge difference!

Are you a fire fighter?

If you don't yet know, one way to find out whether you are spending a lot of time fighting fires is to have a look at the following analogy. Many of us are probably familiar with Stephen Covey's four-quadrant model in *The Seven Habits of Highly Effective People*, about what to spend time on.

The approach works for email too. You receive four basic types of email:

Critical and Urgent. Usually email from someone higher in power, like your boss or an important customer, and the required action is part of your job. It arrives in your inbox, and you have to deal with it immediately.

Critical and Not Urgent. Email that helps you to advance your goals, projects or business, and/or the required action is part of your job. Although it arrives in your inbox, the feeling of urgency is lower, because there is probably no direct action required. You are in charge here, and you need the information to advance your objectives.

Not Critical and Urgent. Someone is facing a deadline and needs your input. In other words, someone else's poor time or project management is put on your plate. The fact that it enters your inbox makes it urgent, it clutters your inbox and you need to take action on it.

Not Critical and Not Urgent. Not actionable or important for your job. This includes spam, social media updates, newsletters, unsolicited offers from a car rental company, and the latest hoax about a dangerous virus. The problem here is that if an email gets into your inbox it creates urgency, even if it isn't urgent. You have to do something with it, and even if this 'only' means deleting or archiving it, it's taking your time and attention away from critical matters.

A quick distinction between Critical and Not Critical email: The first helps you advance your goals, projects, personal development, or business, or is part of your job description. The second doesn't.

If you had to describe the time you spend on the mix of emails in your inbox, what would it look like? On which part of the quadrant do you spend the most time?

> **EXERCISE**
>
> First estimate the total time you spend daily in your inbox.
>
> Then put a percentage in each quadrant that reflects the estimated time you spend on it.
>
> So if you put the total time you spend in your inbox at 100%, what percentage do you roughly spend on 1. Critical and Urgent email, 2. Critical and Not Urgent, 3. Not Critical and Urgent, and finally 4. Not Critical and Not Urgent emails?

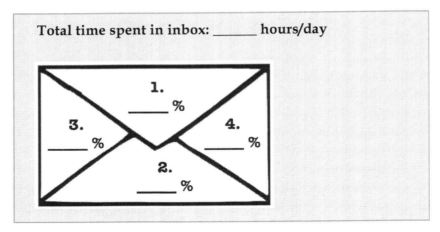

Or are you a business builder?

One important indicator of whether you are a business builder or a fire fighter is the percentage you put in quadrant 2. First of all, people who are in charge of their inbox and use their email just as a tool rather than a replacement for communication spend a significantly smaller amount of time per day in their inbox.

But of the time they do spend on email, they spend a large percentage in quadrant 2. Since this represents the emails that help them to advance their goals, projects, personal development, or business, they know that time spent here will pay out many times over.

What differentiates these business builders from fire fighters is that they have a clear sense of direction. They know what is important. They know what kind of results they desire in their lives and in their business. That's the only way to prevent them from diving into responding everything marked as urgent. The urgent things are often those things that keep us away from focusing on what is important. And they also represent someone else's lack of time management ability.

Do you know what you would like to accomplish in your business? What is important to achieve? What results you desire?

EXERCISE

What do you really want or need to accomplish this year? Just close your eyes for a minute and think: "If I would look back a year from now, what results would I like to have achieved?" Of course you don't have to limit yourself to the business arena. If there are important results to achieve in your personal life, add them to the list.

Then look at what you need to accomplish this month as a first milestone towards your year's goals. Then at what you need to do this week to accomplish the goals for this month. And finally, what do you need to do today as a first step towards achieving your goals for this week.

This Year	This Month	This Week	Today

Now have a look at the list of things you would like to accomplish. If you compare these results to the messages in your inbox, is there a match or a gap? Are the emails a map of your priorities? If you're like I was, there's probably a big gap. Most inboxes do not reflect the priorities that people claim to have.

CHAPTER THREE

The Most Precious Asset: Your Attention

"The most precious gift we can offer anyone is our attention."
– Thich Nhat Hanh

The quality of concentration

Thich Nhat Hanh, Zen master and founder of Plum Village, a Buddhist monastery in France, teaches mindfulness in many of his books. Mindfulness is the ability to be fully present in what you are doing; to pay attention to every little detail. If you are drinking a cup of tea, you are completely aware of each sip, the temperature of the water, the smell of the tea and the texture of the cup. If you take a bite from a cookie, you taste every little bit of it, savoring it in your mouth.

You could say that with mindfulness, your time and attention are one hundred percent aligned. If you spend time on something – for example, on a conversation with your team member – your attention is focused on that conversation as well. And being mindful means you don't let yourself get distracted by an email that pops up on your screen, or by a ringing phone.

According to research[3] by David Meyer, a psychology professor at the University of Michigan, productivity is actually hindered when people try to accomplish two things (or more) at once. Meyer reports that people who switch back and forth between tasks, like working on a project and checking emails, may spend up to 50% more time on those tasks than if they work on them separately, completing one before starting the other.

The most effective way to use your most precious asset – your attention – is to combine it with your time. Becoming a master in creating undisturbed moments that let you concentrate on what you want to accomplish is an invaluable for good management.

Why attention is such a precious asset

In the current knowledge intensive economy, the two most important natural assets you can make use of are your time and your attention.

First of all, you can decide whether or not to spend time on something, and during this time you can display your skills, knowledge and expertise. And alongside spending your time, you can decide to pay attention to something. Think of attention as a highlighter. As you read through a section of text in a book, the highlighted parts stand out, helping you focus on that area. Attention enables you to 'tune out' information, sensations and perceptions that are not relevant at a given moment, and instead focus your energy on what is important.

My neighbor in Spain is a carpenter. For him, carpentry seems easy. If he wants to make a new chair, he devotes his time to that task. And then he directs his attention to the pieces of wood, the sharp saw and the chisel. If he didn't align his time and attention, he would probably have an unstable chair and be missing a couple of fingers.

But for you and me, who spend a lot of time staring at computer screens and dealing with endless interruptions and distractions, it doesn't seem that simple to keep hold attention on the task at hand.

The constant fight for your attention

The following is not news. The volume of external stimuli we process increases every day. Count the number of traffic signs on the road, items in a store, channels on your TV, search results from Google, conversations with colleagues, and emails in your inbox. Everyone and everything is constantly screaming and fighting for your attention. On how many devices can you now receive emails? And how many of these do you use? With my email hooked up to my iPad, phone and laptop, I count three.

Did you know that by default most email clients check the server for new messages once every five minutes? And given how prolifically we communicate, chances are that it will find a new message every time it checks the server. That means a whopping 120 distractions during a 10 hour workday – only from email.

Add to this all the other distractions vying for your attention – such as reports, meeting minutes, market shares, customer data, PR campaigns, CVs, product information, and P&Ls, to name just a few – and you begin to realize you need to build strong walls to protect yourself from distraction.

Consider this: when an accident happens, it is most often due to a misalignment between time and attention. Driving a car (time) + having a fight on the phone (attention) = crash!

How many 'crashes' have you experienced in your business so far due to this phenomenon?

Finite and irreplaceable

Both your time and your attention are finite. And they're both irreplaceable. There is only a given number of hours in a day, and you can't effectively do two things at the same time. We'll come back to this later, but multi-tasking is a myth. A very unproductive one. You can only pay your attention to one thing at a time. Of course you can switch quickly from your computer screen to your phone to the colleague who entered your room and back to your screen, but it's still one thing at a time. If you try to have a conversation on the phone and type an email at the same time, your performance in one of the two (probably both) will be below par – and that's putting it mildly.

"There is time enough for everything in the course of the day, if you do but one thing at once, but there is not time enough in the year, if you will do two things at a time." - Lord Chesterfield

Great managers and leaders master the art of paying attention, the ability to shift their attention, and, more broadly, to exercise judgment about what topics are worthy of their attention. People who have achieved great things often credit their success with a finely honed skill for paying attention. When asked about his particular genius, Isaac Newton responded that if he had made any discoveries, he owed it "more to patient attention than to any other talent."[4]

The myth of multi-tasking

One way of dealing with the ongoing flow of emails is to handle them while on the phone, in a meeting, or talking to someone. Or while you're at home with your kids or your partner. Sitting at the table with your daughter to talk about her day at school, while quickly checking a new email. You might think you're good at multi-tasking. And look around, you're not the only one.

25

Unfortunately, multi-tasking is a myth[5]. The human brain just can't do it. When it comes down to the ability to pay attention, the brain only focuses on concepts sequentially; it can't focus on two things at once. In fact, the brain must disengage from one activity in order to engage in another. It takes several tenths of a second for the brain to make this switch. As such we are biologically incapable of processing inputs simultaneously.

Multi-tasking (or attempting to) might also be taking a toll on the economy. One study[6] by researchers at the University of California at Irvine monitored interruptions among office workers; they found that workers took an average of 25 minutes to recover from interruptions such as phone calls or answering emails and return to their original tasks. Just translate all that recovery time into money.

And lastly, multi-tasking happens to be addictive, which means that it leads to more of the same behavior. John Ratey, an associate professor at Harvard, observed[7] workers who are compulsively drawn to the constant stimulation provided by incoming data. Influenced by the fast pace of modern life and the constant use of technology, they have developed shorter attention spans. They become frustrated with long term projects or activities that require intense concentration.

"They're suckers for irrelevancy," says Clifford Nass, Communication Professor at Stanford University[8]. "Everything distracts them."

Have you had enough? Is this a way of working you want to foster? Would you like to be a manager who lacks the attention span to create winning strategies? Would you like to contribute to the inefficiency of meetings because you need to check your email?

Respect your time

What you spend your time and attention on says a lot about who you are and what you want to accomplish. I once talked with a man who was financially free and didn't have to work for money any more. He told me that for him, the driver to become rich was the notion that time is more important than money: "I can always make more money, but I can never make more time."

At work, we treat time as a commodity resource rather than a precious metal. Managers disrupt the concentration of their team members by sending loads of emails filled with small, irrelevant tasks. Colleagues use the fact that emails are so easy to send to postpone actions to the last minute and then request miracles from the receivers to meet their deadlines. Leadership teams don't create the clarity and alignment needed to fully empower their employees, resulting in rework and confusion. And finally, we don't respect our own time by wasting the most productive hours of the day scrolling through emails, or by attending long, boring meetings without taking action to change something.

Respecting your time means making choices. You cannot do everything. You have to know what you want or need to accomplish, like you described in the previous exercise. Only then can you make a priority call; decide whether the request you just received will help you advance your goals and objectives, or if it is simply a distraction. One time-costly error we make is to think that each email in our inbox needs a proper reply. It doesn't work. The world will keep sending you emails, but you have to consciously decide which ones to deal with and which ones to disregard.

That all sounds very nice, but I don't have time to think about all that. I have still so many things to do today and after that I have a full inbox to deal with...

The fulfillment of completion

The reason so many people report being overwhelmed or even burned out at work is not so much the number of hours they work, but the fact that they spend too many of those hours juggling too many things at the same time.

I was coaching a manager who was a clear example of this. A desk full of unfinished projects, a computer screen with twelve programs open and an inbox with 91 emails (which she had proudly brought down from 278). She was not so much overwhelmed by the inflow of projects and information, but by the stacking up of projects and information as a result of not completing anything.

Assuming you don't crash, the biggest cost is to your productivity. It's a simple consequence of splitting your attention so that you're partially engaged in multiple activities but rarely fully engaged in any one. And, as we've seen before, you're increasing the time it takes to finish that task by an average of 25-50%.

Completion is the fuel for productivity. Here is a powerful exercise to get you into the habit of completing a task. List all the projects that are now on your plate. Determine what stage each project is at:

Stage 1. You may have decided to start it, but not yet acted on it.

Stage 2. You are working on it.

Stage 3. You have completed it.

Now, first decide if you want to continue with a project. For a project that has been dragging on for a long time, it may be a relief to decide to stop or delegate it. If you want or need to complete the project though, think about a small action step that will bring the cycle into motion again. Enjoy the energy and the sense of achievement that come when you keep things moving through the cycle. And don't forget to celebrate each completion before you rush to the next project.

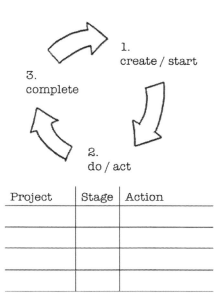

Project	Stage	Action

You can create time

This may seem like a contradiction to what I've said before, but if you look at the amount of time you waste on multi-tasking, interruptions and distractions, there is in fact a lot of time to create. The way to create time, though, is a bit different than you might think.

What I hear most often when working with managers is "that is a great idea, and the moment I have half an hour I will do it." The problem is, you will never have half an hour.

The only way to do the things you want to do is to do them without having the time for it. Read that again. If you know it is of vital importance that you spend two hours – undisturbed – on thinking about the best consumer strategy to recuperate market share, you need to go to your local cafe on Friday morning, order a coffee and think about it.

When my wife and I started our firm, one of our goals was to live and work abroad for three months per year. Having experienced the inspiring effect of changing environments, and the fact that we always returned refreshed and full of brilliant new ideas after a 'workiday', we knew this was vital for our business success. But how on earth could I find a month free between the meetings, appointments and projects that were in my agenda? I couldn't.

So, the only way that I could accomplish this goal was to block off a month – let's say half a year in advance – and book the tickets as a kind of security. It was amazing to see how easy it was after that decision to say to a client "I'm abroad then, but I can make it two weeks later." Another thing we added to out-smart our agenda was always to have our next month abroad secured before we took off for the current month.

The moment you plan the activities that are really important to you in your agenda, all other activities will adjust themselves perfectly around the important ones.

A personal note on attention

Of course, being fully engaged with what you are doing is a quality that won't just benefit you in your business. One of the reasons I started my own consulting firm 11 years ago was to be with our first-born son. Before he arrived I was a member of the leadership team for a huge multinational. However, being a father and a director seemed an impossible combination for me. So I decided to quit my job and start my own firm so I could spend more time with my son.

I will never regret this decision. Now I have two boys, whose early years I have been a big part of. However, I realize that being physically in the same room doesn't necessarily mean I am with them. If my mind is on my next project, or if I'm working on my laptop and answering questions without looking up, I am not engaged in our relationships.

The most important reason my client had to tackle his email overload was so he could really be with his wife and two daughters in the evening, instead of being at home answering his email.

If you become a master of paying attention, and engage fully in what you are doing at any given moment – in other words, if you align your time and your attention – the quality of your life will improve dramatically.

EXERCISE

When you've finished reading this chapter, try to be fully present with what you are doing for the next hour. If you stand up to get a glass of water, taste every sip; notice the freshness of the water and the coldness of the glass. If you have a conversation with your partner or colleague, look her in the eyes, listen to what she says, and notice the color of the clothes she is wearing.

Be aware of your attention.

CHAPTER FOUR

The M.A.I.L. System: Four Steps to Master Your Inbox

"Improvement usually means doing something that we have never done before." – Shigeo Shingo

Treat your inbox as an airport hub

How do you use your inbox? As a meeting point for all incoming email, as a to-do list, or as a follow-up list? Do you prioritize what you will be working on? Or do you do all of the above?

The most important reason for your overflowing inbox is the fact that you treat the inbox incorrectly. Your inbox is your IN-box. Not your STORAGE-box, or your TO-DO-box. It's a place where all email directed to yourname@yourcompany.com will enter your reality. And once it has appeared in your inbox, you need to make a decision about what to do with it, and get it out of your inbox as soon as possible.

The best analogy of your inbox is running an airport hub. All kinds of people (emails) enter your airport building (inbox) and you have to set up a system to select which people should go to what terminal; in the fastest way possible – so they can get to their planes – and with minimum delays. If you keep pushing them around, you don't make money; actually you lose it.

There are different challenges to face. Some people carry heavy suitcases (attachments) that disrupt the logistical efficiencies. Some people obviously don't have the intention to fly (spam), so you have to set up systems to stop them (spam filters) or they will enter your hub again. All the rest need to pass security.

At security, you check if everyone's boarding cards are correct (emails that you have to deal with and are part of your job). If not, they should be stopped at security and directed to border control (the delete area). Of course you want to set up procedures to avoid these types of travelers disrupting the security queue in future (rules and filters). If travelers aren't flying the same day (emails that don't require immediate action), they can be directed to a waiting room (read later or one of your folders). And travelers whose boarding cards are correct and have a flight that departs the same day (email that is part of your job and you need to act on) should go to the gate (one of your action areas).

The only way to make your airport hub a success is to keep people moving and the entrance area and terminals as empty as possible. If security doesn't do a good job, the queue will grow and people will get frustrated. Similarly, if one of the planes is delayed (you don't work on your actions), the gate will become packed with angry people, and you'll have to deal with the consequences.

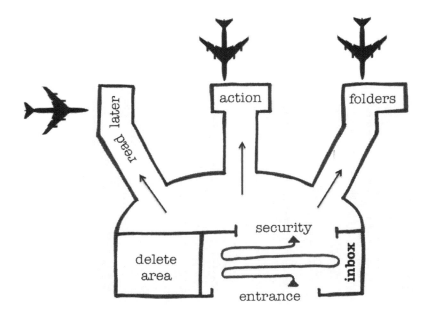

Email overload has nothing to do with the number of emails you receive

Email overload occurs when there is no movement in your inbox and emails are stacking up. The queue grows and grows, until it reaches a point where you lose control.

Actually, email overload has nothing to do with the number of emails you receive every day, but rather with your capability to process them quickly. I have worked with people who receive more than 200 emails a day, and are perfectly in control of keeping things moving. And I have seen people who receive just 10 emails a day, but leave them stacking in what becomes a full inbox.

Of course, if you receive 200 emails a day it's more challenging to keep your inbox manageable, but the habits that support you in keeping things moving are the same regardless of the amount of incoming email.

The M.A.I.L. System™

The process I developed to master my inbox – which has since been used successfully by thousands of people to control their email, create time and spend it instead on activities that really make a difference – is built on four steps:

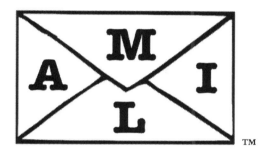

M – Mirrors and Mindsets

A – Actions and Automation

I – Implementation and Integration

L – Leverage and Liberation

This M.A.I.L. system provides you with a complete approach to change the habits that are required to reclaim your inbox, and also to implement and integrate these habits into your daily work. Each M.A.I.L. step will support you on your journey towards mastering your inbox, which is not as difficult as it might seem.

After successfully implementing the four steps, you can manage your inbox in 15 minutes or less, and you can have an empty inbox at least once a day. Let's go through them quickly, one by one.

Step 1. Mirrors and Mindsets

The first M.A.I.L. step is to have a close look in the mirror. What email culture are you part of? What is your current email behavior? And what beliefs do you hold about managing your inbox?

If you want to achieve something new in life, something you didn't have before but would certainly like to have, you have to take into account two types of habit. There are supportive habits, which will help you achieve your goal, and non-supportive habits, which will keep you where you are right now. If you want to lose weight, you can go to the gym three times a week – a supportive habit – or you can take seconds at dinner – a non-supportive habit that will not move the scale in the direction you desire.

Please note that I'm not talking about good or bad habits; there are just supportive and non-supportive habits.

Now, before you can change any non-supportive habits, you need to be clear about what these habits are, where they come from and what underlying beliefs led to these habits. Only then can you successfully address them and make the change to more supportive habits.

So in Mirrors and Mindsets, we create powerful new habits and beliefs with regards to dealing with your time, your inbox and your email. Exactly as Michael Jackson sang, we start with the man (or woman) in the mirror, take a look at ourselves and make the change.

Step 2. Actions and Automation

The second M.A.I.L. step explores the strategies to get to an empty inbox. How can you reduce the flow of incoming emails? What actions could you take with each new email that enters your inbox? What to do with the current backlog of email that is stuck in your inbox?

If your bathtub is overflowing, what's the first you do? You switch off the tap! Only then do you start cleaning up and looking for ways to prevent this happening again. The same is true of your inbox. First, we will look for ways to reduce the flow of incoming email into your inbox. Filters and rules will prove to be important tools to automate this process.

The next question is what should you do with each new email that does enter your inbox? Remember the security gate at the airport hub? We will discuss the two main principles for dealing efficiently with all the incoming emails. One is to 'touch' them only once, as David Allen says in his book *Getting Things Done*, and the other is to select and apply one of five possible actions.

The last element of this M.A.I.L. step is dealing with your backlog and cleaning up all the emails that have become trapped in your inbox. Depending on your situation, this might be a process that will take some time, but you will get there.

Step 3. Implementation and Integration

The third step is where you take control. The good news is that you are fully in charge of what you can achieve with *The 15-Minute Inbox*. This is probably not the first book you have read about improving a situation in your life. And it's no different to the others, in the sense that you have to implement the new approaches. If I could, I would do the work for you, but since you're in control, positive change will only happen in your inbox if you change the non-supportive habits you have today into supportive habits that will help you tomorrow.

In the Implementation and Integration step, you will find all the support you need to implement the new habits that will enable you to control your inbox, and to integrate them into your daily behavior. In my experience, it takes a couple of days to a week to really clean up your inbox, including eliminating your backlog. However, to turn your old non-supportive habits into new supportive ones, and to spend no more than 15 minutes managing your inbox every day, will take a bit longer. Research[9] shows that it takes an average of two to three months to practice new habits and set up structures that remind you of those habits until they become familiar.

Finally, the Implementation and Integration step will deal with situations when email goes wrong. When should you not use email? How can you deal with an email that upsets you? And what can you do when an email ends up in a disaster?

Step 4. Leverage and Liberation

Free at last! With your newly acquired skills and habits, you will be able to create extra time each day. Time you used to spend on inefficient email management, you can now dedicate to your business, or to something else that is important to you.

But first of all, how would your life become easier if the people around you would all apply your new email behavior? How can you leverage the email concepts you have learned, and train the people in your team to master their inboxes?

In this M.A.I.L. step, you will not only explore the possibilities of what you can do now you are liberated from your daily email burden, but you will create a powerful plan to actually achieve the results you're really after in life. I will introduce a proven successful planning methodology, which has helped me personally for over 12 years, enabling me to live my life the way I want to.

How to use this system

You are probably very busy, and may have a lot of emails to deal with before you even have time to finish reading this book. And I'm sure you're tempted to jump straight into action mode. This is fine; you can read this book and learn the steps in the M.A.I.L.™ system in whatever order works for you.

However, I do have one suggestion: If you want to achieve a lasting result – in other words, spend a maximum of 15 minutes managing your inbox to achieve an empty inbox at least once a day, every day – you need to go through the whole process, particularly the Mirrors and Mindsets and Implementation and Integration steps.

The M.A.I.L. system presents an interactive process. You will learn to interact better with your inbox. If you have access to your inbox while reading this book, you will improve your results dramatically. During Mirrors and Mindsets, it's great if you can make a self-assessment of your email behavior based on the facts in front of you. And when dealing with Actions and Automation, you probably want to try a couple of the suggestions immediately to see the instant effect. So access to your inbox is great, but if it's not possible don't worry. The same rules apply when you go to your inbox later.

When can I expect results?

Most people who apply this system completely clean up their inboxes – including enormous backlogs in most cases – in a couple of days. But we're in this for the long haul; after three years of being clean, I am still optimizing my relationship with my inbox.

It's a continuous journey that positively affects all the areas where the flow of information tends to be overwhelming. Creating new rules and filters, becoming better and better at deleting emails instead of archiving everything, opting out of newsletters and distracting notifications, and reducing the number of platforms where you can access your emails all make a positive contribution.

You don't have to travel alone on this journey

Before we take off, one last warning: There are no shortcuts, quick wins or silver bullets. Like in all other areas in your life, the level of success you achieve in managing your inbox depends on you. This is great news, because it means you are completely in control of the outcome.

At the same time, the fact that you are in complete control is probably the exact reason you have not always achieved what you wanted. If you don't implement the steps, or adapt your habits to treat your email differently, not a lot will change.

The good news is you're not alone on this journey. To support you in changing and integrating the habits you need to control your inbox, you can use the unique '30-Day Reminder Service'; an exclusive daily reminder to keep you in the driver's seat. You'll find out more about how to access this service in the Implementation and Integration step. (If you want to skip ahead now, check out www.15MinuteInbox.com/30Days).

And to help you follow up on your personal plan on how to make the next 12 months your best year ever, I'll introduce you to some powerful software and supportive online materials in the Leverage and Liberation step.

So, when you're ready, please fasten your seat belt, stow your tray table, and make sure your seat is in the upright position.

Enjoy the journey!

Step 1:

M is for Mirrors and Mindsets

Before you can decide what kind of behavior will support you in controlling your inbox, you need to have a clear understanding of your current behavior. Where does it come from? Why do you keep it intact?

In this first M.A.I.L. step, we will explore the origin of your current email behavior.

Although you would probably rather jump into action immediately, you need to work on your mindset if you want a lasting result.

CHAPTER FIVE

The Email Culture You are Part of

"The man who follows the crowd will usually get no further than the crowd. The man who walks alone is likely to find himself in places no one has ever been." – Alan Ashley-Pitt

The impact of culture

The culture you belong to has a big impact on who you are as a person, on what you believe, the language you use, how you dress, and many more things. There are a number of ways to describe culture, but my favorite definition is this: "A culture is a set of beliefs that governs behavior."

We are part of many cultures. In fact, during any normal day you can join several different cultures – familiar and new. If you decide to take the train because your car has broken down, you enter the culture of people who travel daily with public transport. And although there is nothing written on the wall, as an observer it seems that there are very clear rules. Where to sit (never next to someone if possible), where to put your coat (in the overhead compartment), where to put your bag (on the seat next to you), how to show your ticket (in a relaxed way, and only when the conductor asks for it), and how to greet other passengers (not at all if possible, hence your bag on the seat next to you).

When you enter your office, you step into another culture, with lots of different unwritten rules; just have a look at a random company's canteen – how people wait in line, how they select their food, in what order they compose their meals, where they sit and don't sit – it all runs according to a culture.

The thing is that it's very hard or almost impossible to observe different cultures when you are a part of them. This only seems possible for someone who is not part of the specific culture they're observing, as they can look at the behavior that belongs to that culture from an objective point of view.

The email culture in an organization

The same is true of email and the email culture you are a part of. The industry you work in, the core values of your organization, and even the competitiveness of the environment can all have an influence on your current email behavior. But the biggest influencer of any culture is the behavioral example of the leadership team.

I work with the leadership teams of organizations in different industries, in different countries, and of different sizes. What I notice is that each company, even if it is part of a multinational organization, has its own distinct culture. What I also notice is that the leadership team always plays a crucial role in shaping this culture. People copy the exact behavior of their bosses and managers, especially in times of stress.

Now, what has a leadership team to do with the email behavior in an organization? A lot.

If a director sends a lot of his emails marked as 'Urgent', he stimulates an environment of ad hoc fire fighting. Everything is vital; everything needs to be dealt with right now. It's unlikely that the people who receive these emails are waiting quietly in their chairs for them to arrive. They are probably working on something else. But when an email pops in, they are forced to drop whatever they are doing and answer their boss's urgent message.

After a while, they start marking the emails they send to their team members as 'Urgent'. And in this way, non-supportive email behavior drips down through the layers of the organization, until it becomes part of its culture.

Examples of email cultures

One of my clients is a public organization that falls under the supervision of the European Commission. As such, politics is part of the organization's DNA. One of the beliefs embedded in their way of working is that you need a written track record of every conversation. Although this might be true for certain legal conversations, it's definitely not necessary for every email exchange that takes place.

Also, given the organization's political origin, their ingrained need to inform people of everything results in endless 'Cc' and 'Reply to All' messages. A lot of employees complain that managing their inbox is almost a whole day's task.

Another client is a multinational company in the fast moving consumer goods industry. The culture is financially driven, and the top management's bonuses often depend on short-term results. You can almost predict the effect on their email behavior: As fast-moving as their products, their emails are short-term focused, and sent in haste, so are not very clearly written. This email behavior leads to in unclear answers and rework. That's exactly what the company was experiencing.

Another client is a small architecture firm. There are 25 employees, all working in the same building, with very short communication lines. If you need something from a colleague, he or she is only sitting two desks away, so you stand up, walk to their desk and ask for it. Because of this, the firm's email culture still reflects what email was meant to be: a carrier of information, not a substitute for all other forms of communication.

The Four-Flap Model™

Let's have another look at the model we discussed in Chapter Two about the different types of email, and on which types you spend your time.

Critical and Urgent. Usually email from someone higher in power, like your boss or an important customer, and the required action is part of your job. It arrives in your inbox, and you have to deal with it immediately.

Critical and Not Urgent. Email that helps you to advance your goals, projects or business, and/or the required action is part of your job. Although it arrives in your inbox, the feeling of urgency is lower, because there is probably no direct action required. You are in charge here, and you need the information to advance your objectives.

Not Critical and Urgent. Someone is facing a deadline and needs your input. In other words, someone else's poor time or project management is put on your plate. The fact that it enters your inbox makes it urgent, it clutters your inbox and you need to take action on it.

Not Critical and Not Urgent. Not actionable or important for your job. This includes spam, social media updates, newsletters, unsolicited offers from a car rental company, and the latest hoax about a dangerous virus. The problem here is that if an email gets into your inbox it creates urgency, even if it isn't urgent. You have to do something with it, and even if this 'only' means deleting or archiving it, it's taking your time and attention away from critical matters.

If we put each of these four types of email onto one of the flaps of an envelope, we get the following model:

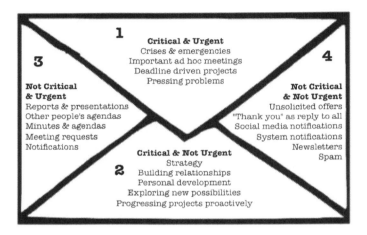

Which flap best describes the email culture in your organization?

What type of email do you most often see arriving?

On which flap do you spend most of your own time?

What type of email do you send most of the time?

If you could eliminate one flap, which one would it be?

As Stephen Covey stated in his *Seven Habits of Highly Effective People*, "If we don't have a clear idea of what is important, of the results we desire in our lives, we are easily diverted into responding to the urgent." The urgent things are often those things that keep us away from focusing on what is important.

When email is a symptom of something much larger

If you are in a management position, email dynamics are a fantastic indicator of what is going on in your team or organization. And very often email is a symptom of something larger.

Have a look at the following situations and see if you recognize any of them - maybe they even apply to your situation.

Flaw in job description

First of all, the amount of email your direct report has to deal with could indicate a flaw in his or her job description. I've seen situations where certain job responsibilities couldn't fit on top of people's current daily workload.

One manager was running a production department with 55 employees. He ran this group properly, until the moment the annual Individual Assessments needed to be written. That meant at least 90 minutes of work per employee, if he wanted to give each one a fair assessment and a personal reward. In order to deal with this peak in workload, he chose to start his day at 5am, giving himself two hours of quiet writing time every morning. He did this for a month.

Of course, it's great if someone finds a way out, but this clearly has a cost, either for the quality of someone's work, or for his or her private life. To solve this particular issue, we talked with HR and agreed to spread the assessments over the year instead of having them all at the same time.

Lack of trust

A clear indicator for lack of trust and open communication in a team, department or organization is the frequent unhealthy use of the Bcc field. The sender of the email puts himself in a peculiar situation by not confronting his colleague directly, but rather talking about her behind her back. It's like gossiping, and we can't trust people who gossip. I mean, next time they might be gossiping about us.

But more importantly, if you are the blind copied recipient, you are now pulled into a 'secret'; you know something about someone that doesn't know that you know. This certainly has an effect on how you will communicate in future with the official recipient of the email. And if you don't act on your new knowledge, you become part of a little conspiracy.

By the way, blind copies are never as blind as you might think. Information that you're not supposed to know tends to pop up at the most inconvenient moments. So to protect your integrity as well as to prevent an environment of distrust, it seems like a good idea not to allow the use of the Bcc field in your teams.

The Cc field can have a similar effect on trust – though more transparent than a Bcc, it can be damaging when people send an email to a colleague with a Cc to you as a manager. If you allow your team members to play this power game to put pressure on colleagues, you will end up with a lot of additional emails in your inbox.

Lack of clarity

Emails that pass by with a lot of people in the Cc field could indicate a lack of clarity about a project or job responsibilities. If it is not clear who needs to be informed about what, and who is responsible for certain decisions, people tend to include everyone in the email. Better to be safe than sorry.

This, of course, is an easy issue to solve. Discuss the topic during a meeting or create the clarity needed and communicate it to your teams.

Lack of empowerment

Another, more serious, cause for the many-people-in-Cc symptom is a lack of empowerment. When the culture in your organization doesn't allow errors to be made, people don't take decisions easily. And if they communicate something via email, they try to cover the 'risk' they took by copying in a lot of other people. Almost to say, if something went wrong, "I've informed you, you knew about it, so you're part of this failure." Or they hope that someone in the Cc list will take a decision or offer support for their idea, making it a 'shared risk'.

The disempowerment issue is something you definitely want to tackle, at least if you appreciate your time. You have people working in a team to create efficiencies, not to create more work for you. And when they don't feel safe taking decisions, the consequences will land on your plate, or in your inbox!

Lack of training

Apart from the issues described above, the most frequent cause of email overload in an organization is a lack of the right skills, habits and training. We just never learned how to deal with so much information on a daily basis. And the skills needed for dealing with information overload are different to those we need for understanding Word or PowerPoint, or even Outlook. Because when it comes to controlling email, it's less about skills, and more about habits!

I haven't worked with many organizations that train or support their people in controlling email and information overload (only one, to be precise). If you are a new hire, it's taken for granted that you can deal with emails and information, and you'll have to find your own way. If you switch jobs or functions, you will encounter the same situation: You have to find your own way.

One of the managers I work with had an overflowing inbox. Since she was new in her function, she didn't yet know what was important and what wasn't. She had particular trouble deciding what to file and what not to. Since she had no clear filing structure, she left all her emails in her inbox; this was not exactly helping her create the job clarity she was looking for.

Again, email overload is not about the amount of email you receive daily. It's about the amount of email that you leave in your inbox, allowing it to stack up and distract your attention, regardless of whether you receive 10 or 200 new emails every day.

Describe the email culture that you are part of

Let's have a look at the email culture you are part of. Try to describe the general culture of how email is used in your whole organization, or more specifically how email is used in your team.

How would you describe the email culture you are part of?

In terms of email use; for what types of communication do people use email? (E.g. project updates, urgent requests, jokes)

_____

_____

_____

_____

In terms of volume; how many emails do people send/receive on average every day?

_____

_____

_____

_____

In terms of urgency; how quickly do people expect answers to emails?

_____

_____

_____

_____

In terms of... (you fill in the gap)

_____

_____

_____

_____

The Culture-Behavior-Beliefs Diabolo

The following model explains the relationship between the culture you are a part of, your own behavior, and your underlying beliefs or mindsets. Culture is the set of beliefs that governs behavior. In other words, if you want to change a culture, ultimately you have to change the beliefs that are underneath it.

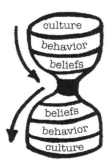

Beliefs are hard to see or notice; it is much easier to notice the resulting behavior caused by those beliefs. Behavior is everything we do or don't do. So, for instance, if I believe I am not good at speaking in public, then my behavior might be that I stumble on stage with shaking knees and a red face. That's something you would notice. Or if I believe that nobody acknowledges my work, I might send a lot of emails using the Cc field to show the world what I'm doing. That's something you would notice.

If you look at the model, you can see the steps you can follow to change or influence a certain culture, or the non-supportive parts of a culture, from move from an old to a new situation. First you explore the culture you are a part of and pick out any non-supportive elements. Then you have a look at your own behavior, and define the actions you take that could be seen as part of this culture. And finally, you look at the underlying non-supportive beliefs and mindsets that you think are true for you or the situation.

Once you have determined the non-supportive (top) part of the diabolo, you cross over to the supportive (bottom) side, but now the other way around. Having identified your non-supportive beliefs and mindsets, and realizing that these are just thoughts you keep thinking, it is possible to create or be aware of supportive beliefs to replace them. These new beliefs will be the basis for your new behavior, and will ultimately influence a new culture.

Who are you in this culture?

"If you wanna make the world a better place, take a look at yourself and then make a change!" - Michael Jackson

The email culture you are part of is one important contributor to your current email behavior. And it's a tough one, I fully agree. Why is it that the observations of new employees are most valuable during the first three months after starting with a new company? Because after that period, they have become part of the culture and view things the same as everybody else does. Email culture can be very demanding in a way, as it seems like you have to comply with the unwritten rules.

But don't fool yourself. It only seems like you have to comply. You don't really have to. And although the email culture might explain your current behavior, it's not an excuse for it. There is a space between experiencing the urge to send an email and actually sending it. In this space you can make a choice. And it is this choice that can make a difference.

Changing the email behavior of your team and your organization slowly but surely begins with you. If everybody around you is using email as their only means of communication, and spending hours every day managing their teams from behind their screens, you have to break the routine. If you receive hundreds of emails that don't add value to your real job, you have to be clear in your expectations.

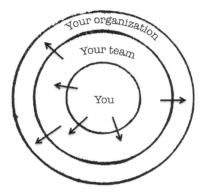

Nobody will make the change for you, whatever it may be. If you want a different email culture, you have to believe, say and do new things yourself.

The beauty of this approach is that you are not dependent on anyone. And it's very contagious, so it won't be long before your team notices the change and adapts their own behavior to incorporate some of your best practices.

CHAPTER SIX

Your Email Behavior

"He who knows others is learned; he who knows himself is wise."
– Lao-tzu, Tao te Ching

Know thyself

As we saw in the previous chapter, if you know the impact of the email culture you are part of, you have the ability to stop it from affecting your behavior. In a way, the culture is shaped by the sum of everyone's individual email behavior, so acting alone there may not be much you can do to change it.

In this chapter, you are going to assess the current situation with regards to your individual email behavior. If you want to travel to a new destination, you need to know where you're coming from, otherwise you can't plan the route. The same is true for your email habits and behavior, especially those that are not supporting you in mastering your inbox.

And just to be clear, I'm not talking about good or bad behavior. There is nothing wrong with the way you have managed your emails before now. It might not always have been effective, or it might have led to an overflowing inbox, but that's all. Try to look at yourself from the perspective of an objective observer, and describe the facts that you notice. Don't start justifying anything.

How does your inbox look?

Let's start with an easy assessment. How does your inbox look? You could almost delegate this step, because you just need to look at the facts that you see in front of you when you look at your inbox. Don't cheat, don't justify, just count.

> *Today's date:*
>
> *Total number of emails in inbox:*
>
> *Number of unread emails in inbox:*
>
> *Number of top-line folders:*
>
> *Total number of folders:*
>
> *Number of different senders (sort on 'Sender' or 'From'):*
>
> *Average number of new emails per day:*
>
> *Time in days between the oldest email in your inbox and today:*

You have just created a small database with a wealth of information that will be your baseline or reference point for measuring your future progress.

How do you 'do email'?

For the next step of your self-assessment you are going to describe a typical email day. You will find several sentences that you can complete to reflect the way you 'do email'. The more detailed the better. For inspiration, I have provided an example with every sentence.

Again, you could delegate this exercise to someone else, because it requires you to observe your behavior just the way it is. Nothing added and nothing left out.

Have fun!

"When I wake up, I pick up my smart phone to switch off the alarm. Then I go to my email program to see what new messages have arrived. I scroll through them quickly, delete the most obvious ones and answer a couple. Then I put my phone back."

"When I wake up ...

_____

_____

_____

_____ _"_

"When I arrive in my office the first thing I do is to start up my computer and open my email program. I scroll through the whole list in my inbox to see if anything needs to be dealt with right now. I start answering an email that requires a longer answer, but keep it open when a new email arrives that I check first. Then I finish the first one, click send and look for the correct folder to archive the original mail. I also go to my Send folder and archive my answer for future reference.

I delete some older emails after quickly reading them to be sure they can go. I go through an attached PowerPoint presentation and click on several links that are included. I spend several minutes browsing the websites they link to. Then I have my first meeting that day."

"When I arrive in my office ...

_____

_____

_____

_____"

"During a meeting I have my laptop with me, or at least my smart phone. I regularly check my emails and craft some quick answers when needed."

"During a meeting...

_____

_____

_____

_____"

"When I come back from a meeting, I first go to my email program and quickly scan the new email to see if anything important needs immediate action. I answer a couple of emails and archive them in their corresponding folders. I delete some obvious emails and start answering one that needs an urgent answer."

"When I come back from a meeting...

_____

_____

_____

_____ "

"During the working day I check my new emails the moment they arrive. I always have my email program open in the background and every time a new email appears, I quickly check it to see if it's something important that needs immediate action."

"During the working day I check my new emails...

_____

_____

_____

_____ "

"When I get home after work I have dinner with my family. After dinner I pick up my phone and check the screen to see if there are any new emails. I answer two of them and put back my phone."

"When I get home after work...

_____

_____

_____

_____ "

"Before I go to sleep, I set the alarm on my phone. I check the few new emails that have arrived in the meantime, quickly answer one, switch off my phone and go to sleep."

"Before I go to sleep...

_____

_____

_____

_____ "

Well done! You have added another set of valuable information to your self-assessment. And again, it doesn't matter if you like what you've written or not, this is just what is. Let's move on to the next step.

How much time do you spend managing your inbox?

This step requires a bit of homework, or best estimating. It's not a bad idea to keep some notes on this question during the next couple of days, so you get a realistic insight to the amount of time you spend managing your inbox. Your answers to the questions in the previous exercise will help you translate your email behavior into time estimates. And you may need a piece of paper, a pen and a calculator (or a spreadsheet) to translate minutes into percentages of your day.

How much time do you spend each day with your inbox open as your main screen (include computer, phone, tablet): _____ hours

Let's set this total time you spend per day working in your in-box as 100%.

What percentage of this time do you spend on:

> *Scrolling through your inbox and scanning subject lines*
>
> *Opening and reading emails*
>
> *Opening and reading attachments or links*
>
> *Answering emails*
>
> *Writing new emails*
>
> *Archiving emails*
>
> *Retrieving archived emails*
>
> *Other inbox related activities (cooling off from an upsetting or frustrating email, waiting for messages to load, restructuring your archive folders, etc.)*

Where do you spend most of your time?
Any surprises?

On to the next step.

How addicted to email are you?

I think it's fair to say that the compulsory behavior that some of us display around email would fit the definition of an addiction. Let's check the following questions[10].

1. When you are in a meeting, how often do check your emails?

□ *Never*
□ *Occasionally*
□ *Often*

2. Outside normal office working hours, how often do you check your work emails?

□ *Never*
□ *Occasionally*
□ *Often*

3. When you are on holiday, how often do you check your work emails?

□ *Never*
□ *Towards the end of the vacation*
□ *Every couple of days*
□ *Once a day*
□ *Twice a day*
□ *Constantly*

4. Do you have all the new email notifications/alerts switched off?

□ *Yes*
□ *No*

5. When you are in the office working at your desk, how often do you check your emails?

□ *Constantly*
□ *Every 30 minutes*
□ *Once an hour*
□ *Every couple of hours*
□ *Two to three times a day*

6. If you have not received many new emails during the day, how do you feel?

☐ *Fine, pleased to be able to get on with the task at hand*
☐ *Concerned that something is wrong*
☐ *Stressed, and call the help desk to make sure my mailbox is working*

7. If the email system crashes, how long before you feel you can no longer work properly?

☐ *A few days*
☐ *About a day*
☐ *Half a day*
☐ *A couple of hours*
☐ *Less than an hour*
☐ *Less than 30 minutes*

8. Do you check your emails during one of the following situations?

☐ *Going to the bathroom*
☐ *In bed*
☐ *During a wedding or funeral*
☐ *Driving*
☐ *Waiting in line at a store*

Just have an honest look at your answers. If these answers were from someone else, and you had to give them a diagnosis, what would the verdict be? Addicted, mildly addicted, or everything under control?

Speed of reply

There is often a difference between what you expect from others and how you behave yourself. In this case, there may be a difference between what you – the sender – expects as an appropriate reply time, and what the recipient considers to be an appropriate reply time,.

How quickly do you normally answer an email that you receive?

☐ *Immediately*
☐ *Within one hour*
☐ *Within half a day*
☐ *Within a day*
☐ *Within a couple of days*

How quickly do you normally expect a reply to an email that you send:

☐ *Immediately*
☐ *Within one hour*
☐ *Within half a day*
☐ *Within a day*
☐ *Within a couple of days*

Is there a gap between your behavior and your expectations of others? Are you putting stricter rules on yourself than on others? What would happen if you gave yourself a bit more time to answer emails?

Irritating email behavior of other people

What irritates and frustrates you most about the email behavior of others? For instance, I hate replies to all, a copy to ten other people, heavy attachments, ten people in the 'To' field, long, vague emails with no clear action points, long legal statements at the bottom of emails that warn me about I-don't-know-what if I receive this mail by accident, long signatures, wacky colors, comic fonts, unclear subject lines, an old subject line with new, unrelated message content, and urgent emails that needed a reply yesterday.

Enough inspiration? Now make your own list and write down all the things that you find irritating. Don't censor. Remember, it's your exercise and honesty will bring its own rewards.

What I don't like / I hate / irritates me about other people's email behavior is:

_____

_____

_____

_____

My own irritating email behavior

We are still in self-assessment mode. And you could have predicted this question would come. So now go through the list you just wrote and compare the irritating behavior of other people to your own behavior by looking through the emails in your Sent folder. Carry out an honest analysis and write down the answers below.

My own irritating email behavior:

_____

_____

_____

_____

That's it for the self-analysis. Well done!

CHAPTER SEVEN

It's All About Your Mindset

"If you hear a voice within you say 'You cannot paint', then by all means paint, and that voice will be silenced." – Vincent Van Gogh

Paradigms, mindsets and beliefs

All our behavior is rooted in paradigms, mindsets and beliefs - whatever you want to call them. We act according to what we believe. If you look at the following dictionary definitions, you'll notice the commonality between the three.

Paradigm: A set of assumptions, concepts, values, and practices that constitutes a way of viewing reality.

Mindset: A fixed mental attitude that predetermines a person's responses to and interpretations of situations.

Belief: A mental acceptance of and conviction in the truth, or validity of something

They are all ingrained in our mind, they're fixed, and they determine the way we view reality and act. And they are there for a reason. If humankind had to change its paradigms every single time something changed, life would be an exhausting or even dangerous undertaking.

However, it's good to realize where our mindsets help us in viewing reality and where they don't.

One nasty element of a paradigm or belief is that it's the truth. At least, it's the truth for you. And what makes it even worse is that you have all the evidence and justification that it's the truth. Maybe you've tried to change your email situation before, but it didn't work. *You see? It is just impossible in our organization.*

So, in order to adjust your behavior to enable you to control your email, you need to understand the dynamics behind mindset and behavior, and the relationship between your mindset and your full inbox.

The relationship between your mindset and your full inbox

Have a look at the model below, which is similar to the bottom part of the diabolo I discussed in Chapter Five.

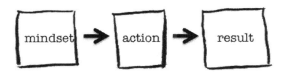

The results you experience in your inbox are a direct consequence of the actions you take, or don't take. In other words, this is about your behavior. If you create clarity for your team members about what their job responsibilities include, and an environment where everyone holds each other accountable for their tasks, you establish a situation where people know exactly who they should contact for what. As a result, email communication is limited, and only takes place between the people who really need to be involved.

On the other hand, if you want to be informed about every piece of communication that is exchanged in your team, your inbox will be overloaded with email, mainly with you in the Cc field. And your team members will complain that you micro-manage them. It's as simple as that.

Now, when you come across situations that have led to undesirable results, it's likely that you'll try to change something about your – or other people's – behavior. For example, you might try to tackle an influx of irrelevant emails by sending out a very detailed document outlining the situations in which you do and don't want to be informed. However, if you don't back this up with consistent actions it still won't work; if you ask about nitty-gritty details during meetings or if you send a lot of emails to follow up on the status of a project, your inbox will remain full. And your team members will keep complaining about their lack of empowerment.

Why?

Maybe you don't trust your team members. Maybe you have a hard time trusting that they can do their jobs properly, or maybe you are afraid. You may fear that they will make a mistake that could backfire on you.

Those are the underlying mindsets. And if you don't change the way you view reality, your results will unfortunately remain the same.

The self-fulfilling prophecy of your mindsets

But why does it seem so difficult to change your mindset?

For one, they are not really tangible. You can't see them, like behavior. You could compare a mindset with the little voice in your head that starts talking when you're quiet for a moment ("What voice, what is he talking about?" - that voice).

The second reason is that you're right about your view of the world. It is the truth. And you're willing to defend it and convince others about the validity of it, because you can prove you're right.

At my level it is impossible to control your inbox, it's just comes with the job. Want to see my inbox to prove my point?

There's the trick. Of course you can prove it. Because the results you see are an exact consequence of your mindsets and paradigms. This means you are always right.

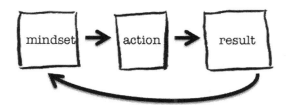

Now, here's the opportunity. If your current mindsets and paradigms drive your current results, proving you are right, then a different mindset might result in a different outcome, therefore fueling a different truth. Or as Henry Ford stated: "Whether you think you can, or you think you can't – you're right."

What are your non-supportive email mindsets?

A good start to identify the non-supportive mindsets that drive your email behavior is to look at the excuses you use to justify your full inbox. They reflect your underlying beliefs perfectly.

Why do I have a full inbox?

Because...

I don't have the time to manage it; there are not enough hours in a day.

I receive too many emails.

I keep everything there so it's my to-do list.

At my level it is impossible to manage; it comes with the job.

I just don't know how to deal with it; I've given up.

Write down your justifications:

_____

_____

_____

_____

Why do I check my mail every time it enters my inbox?

Because...

You never know if something important needs to be dealt with now.

I want to know what the email is about.

I can't resist the temptation to have a look.

Maybe it's from my boss.

To be honest, I like to be needed.

Write down your justifications:

_____

_____

_____

_____

Have a look at your list and recognize that you are probably right about all the justifications you wrote down, and you can probably provide me with plenty of proof. Now realize that they are all just mindsets: Non-supportive mindsets, if your goal is to change the size of your inbox and the time you spend on managing your email.

Changing your email mindsets

Since mindsets and beliefs are nothing more than thoughts that you had repeatedly, until you found enough evidence to accept them as true, why not choose different thoughts?

For instance, I really believe it is possible to manage my inbox. And that I don't need to answer every single email that enters my inbox. And that email is a tool that helps me to advance my goals and objectives instead of hindering their accomplishment. And that I can deal with all my emails quickly even if I don't look at my inbox for a full day. And that if something is really important and urgent, someone will call me instead. I have figured out that I can reduce the flow of incoming email.

These mindsets support me in my current email behavior and hence in reducing the size of my inbox. I have an empty inbox at least once a day, I have dramatically reduced the flow of incoming email, and I don't spend more than 15 minutes managing my inbox each time I consciously decide to work on my emails. And over the same period I achieved these email results, I almost doubled my revenue each consecutive year. It's clear to me that spending my time and attention on the activities that really add value pays out big time.

Now, have a look at the non-supportive mindsets that you have listed above. What supportive mindsets could you create instead?

Supportive mindsets that will help me to control my email and create more time:

_____

_____

_____

_____

Of course, I realize it's not as easy as this. Your email world will not change by doing this exercise and saying, "I believe I can manage my inbox." First, you need to adjust your behavior and see some evidence to support these new mindsets before you can even start to believe them. And your old, existing mindsets are still much more powerful than these new ones – that voice will be showing you all its evidence to support your old beliefs.

But you simply have to start with this step and try to consciously apply more supportive mindsets when you are working on your new email behavior. Proof of a different constructive relationship with your inbox will develop over time, especially if you are open to it.

Picturing the future

Why do you want to be in control of your email? How would it feel if you were to have an empty inbox at least once every day? And what would you do if you created an additional hour or more each day by eliminating your inefficient email habits?

The following exercise is a powerful tool to help you visualize the answers to these questions and picture the future. When you have taken care of your mindset, the visualization of the results you want to realize is a crucial step towards actually achieving them. Our brains are extremely powerful at focusing on the information we need to achieve what we want.

Visualization is a technique used by many top athletes. Golf legend Jack Nicklaus never hit a shot before visualizing every little detail:

"I never hit a shot, not even in practice, without having a very sharp, in-focus picture of it in my head. First I see the ball where I want it to finish, nice and white and sitting up high on the bright green grass. Then the scene quickly changes, and I see the ball going there: its path, trajectory, and shape, even its behavior on landing. The next scene shows me making the kind of swing that will turn the previous images to reality."

Take a piece of paper and draw a circle in the middle. In the center write the question 'Why do I want to have an empty inbox?' Now add a couple of spokes to the circle. Write down the first answer that pops into your mind at the end of a spoke. Then listen to the next answer and write it at the end of the next spoke. Repeat this until you have a full wheel of answers drawn up.

You can of course always add spokes later on.

Before you begin, make sure you start from a supportive mind-set!

Here's my example:

Do the same for each of the following questions as well:

How would it feel to have an empty inbox once a day?

What would I do if I created an extra hour every day with supportive email habits?

Let's take action

With a supportive mindset and a clear picture of the results you want to achieve in the future, you are well prepared for the second step of the M.A.I.L. system: Actions and Automation. Here you will learn about the 'doing' that is needed to reclaim your inbox and your life.

Remember that you can always come back to this section. If the results that you're after don't show up fast enough, it's a good idea to check your underlying mindsets. But for now, let's get going!

Step 2:

A is for Actions and Automation

Now, it's time for action!

In this second M.A.I.L. step, we will discuss the strategies to help you get to an empty inbox. How can you reduce the flow of incoming emails? What actions could you take with each new email that enters your inbox? And what to do with the current backlog of emails stuck in your inbox?

I highly recommend you have access to your inbox while going through the Actions and Automation step, so you can apply the different methods you have learnt immediately.

CHAPTER EIGHT

Tame the Flow of Incoming Email

"There is nothing so useless as doing efficiently that which should not be done at all." – Peter F. Drucker

Overflowing bath tub

Imagine that you are sitting in your living room enjoying a cup of tea. Suddenly, some drops of water fall down from the ceiling in your cup. Looking up to the ceiling you immediately realize what is happening. The bath you are running is overflowing. You run upstairs, open the door of the bathroom, and switch off the tap. Only then do you start cleaning up the mess, and look for the reason behind the overflow to avoid this disaster happening again in the future.

The same goes for your inbox[11]. Before we explore the actions you can take to move emails out of your inbox, we need to look at which taps we can switch off. And although this might not have an immediate effect on the current size of your inbox, it will have a huge effect on the future flow of incoming emails.

Basically, the main principle behind taming email inflow is to only allow relevant emails to enter your inbox. This means relevant as in part of your job and requiring immediate action. All other emails should be directed immediately to their designated folders, without you having to see them in your inbox.

Turn off email notifications

Many people still have email notification activated. This means that every time a new email arrives in their inbox, which is once every five minutes by default, a visual or audible signal is distracting them user from their work. Every five minutes in a 10-hour working day results in 120 interruptions.

Even if it doesn't show up in your inbox, consider anything that distracts your attention when you look at your screen as something to eliminate. In that sense the notification of a new email is as toxic as the email in your inbox itself.

@CTION: Switch this notification functionality off if this applies to you.

Another notification that you should not use is the Read Receipt option. This is literally asking for additional email in your inbox. And besides this, it doesn't make you very popular. Receiving an email with the message "The sender asked to be notified when you read this message" always gives me a strange feeling. *Doesn't she trust me? Am I supposed to act on this immediately now she knows I've read it? I'd better not send the receipt. But then she might think I never read it and call me instead… Maybe I'd better send the receipt later today.*

(By the way, do you notice the time wasted by this little conversation in the recipient's head? Be nice to your inbox and be nice to the recipients of your emails. It'll save you all time.)
@CTION: Switch off the Read Receipt if you use this as a default option. If you don't use it, keep it like that.

Eliminate spam

The spam filters used in most organizations today filter out almost all unwanted email that tries to lure the recipient into buying certain blue pills, cheap medicines, or penny stocks, or, worse, to sneakily introduce a virus into their systems. Luckily the filters do a good job; recent research[12] revealed that 88 – 92% of all global email traffic is caused by spam.

This is a topic that doesn't require much discussion. Make sure you have the best virus and spam filters available on the market, and if you still receive spam via your business email, contact your IT help desk and see what you can do to prevent this in future. You do not want to receive any spam in your inbox; even if it only takes a split second to notice and delete spam, it still requires unnecessary decisions and actions from you.

@CTION: Check your inbox and Deleted or Trash folder to see if you still receive spam. If so, take appropriate action. Call the IT help desk, update your spam settings, or invest in a solid spam blocker.

Separate your business and personal email

A small note on preventing spam. Never ever use your company's email address for anything other than business related communication. Apart from the fact that it is illegal – your company's email address is property of your company – it is a surefire way to fill your inbox with unwanted emails.

I made this mistake in the past myself, and I still pay the consequences. It seems that once your email address is in one of those spam databases, it's doomed to stay there; you can't just unsubscribe from the global spam database.

Make sure that you use your corporate email address only for work-related communication. That means for communicating with your colleagues, your suppliers or service providers and your clients. For all other communication you should have a separate personal email address, like Gmail or Yahoo.

Most people that I work with make this distinction. However, sometimes I run into an inbox where business-related emails are mixed up with Facebook and Twitter updates, newsletters about the latest wine collections, bank statements, eBay purchases, and airline offers. This provides a great opportunity for reducing the flow of incoming emails.

@CTION: If you receive non-business-related emails at work, open a private email account. Change the email address for all non-business-related emails that you receive now in your inbox. Maybe this requires a bit of time investment now, but it will save you a lot of time in the future.

Opt out

I would be the last person to deny the usefulness of social networking platforms like LinkedIn. I meet a lot of interesting people in the virtual world that I would have never been able to meet in the real world. However, LinkedIn, Facebook, Twitter and all the other networks have a tendency to over communicate, telling us about every single activity that takes place in the virtual world.

But we don't need to receive all those notifications. You can reduce your email inflow by opting out of all the notifications from your social media networks.

@CTION: Go to LinkedIn, Twitter, Facebook and any other applicable social media platform, and update your notification requirements. (Or, if you still want to receive some notifications, change the email address to your personal email.)

Another area where you can reduce the flow of incoming emails is in the world of newsletters. Over time you might have accumulated a lot of subscriptions for newsletters that once contained an interesting piece of information. Luckily, most of these newsletters have a very easy unsubscribe link at the bottom.

@CTION: Scroll through your inbox and see if there are any opportunities where you can unsubscribe from mailing lists. After that go through your Deleted or Trash folder and do the same; you will probably find even more opportunities for unsubscribing here.

In the future, for any new newsletter or notification that you receive, make the effort to unsubscribe so you won't receive it again.

Change the server settings

This is a scary one, though very powerful. Did you know that the default setting for checking the server for new emails is set to either continuous or every five minutes? Given the normal flow of email and a 10-hour workday, that means 120 interruptions per day. I changed this setting to once every hour, therefore I have only ten interruptions and, more importantly, it forces me to treat my emails in batches, because they enter my inbox in batches.

The reason I said this is a scary one is that you don't want to disconnect. Maybe something important will enter your inbox. True? I have heard many excuses as to why making this change is a bad idea.

Well, just think about it. What happens if you are traveling by plane? You don't have access. And what if you are in an important meeting, one where you can't check your emails? Or let's say you're ill – what happens then? Do you manage, or do you not manage? The world continues to turn. You will be fine without reading your emails for one hour.

Still too scary? Start with setting the server to check for new emails once every 20 minutes, or once every 30 minutes. But face the fact that the reasons you may have for not making the change are the exact same reasons you have an issue with email management. You think you are indispensable and you don't want to miss any information - even if this leads to stress or an overloaded inbox.

@CTION: If possible (sometimes you can't because of company settings) go to your server settings and change the "check for new messages" timings at least to the next level. At least.

> *Check for new messages:*
>
> ☐ *Every minute*
> ☐ *Every 5 minutes*
> ☐ *Every 15 minutes*
> ☐ *Every 30 minutes*
> ☐ *Every hour*
> ☐ *Manually*

This is a big step. And although you will not receive fewer emails, you will receive fewer interruptions. Make sure you treat yourself if you have taken this step!

Use chat for short conversations

One type of communication that is responsible for a lot of email traffic is the short conversation that takes place via the email server. Email is not an appropriate tool for the quick, short messages that are exchanged between people. Take a look at the structure of an email, with its subject, date, sender, recipient, signature and previous messages at the bottom. Doesn't it just looks a little bit over-designed to carry only the words 'okay', 'yes', 'will do', or 'thanks'?

There is definitely a need for a chat platform for teams or project groups; such a platform could dramatically reduce the flow of emails. I frequently make use of the different chat platforms that are on the market, such as Skype, Twitter and Facebook, for short conversations with people. This is a perfect method of communicating if you just need to ask for a link, find a piece of information, or ask a quick question.

There are many options available on the market for chat platforms in company environments, and it might be worthwhile looking into the possibilities. You could also use an existing platform such as Skype. Team members just need to download Skype and create a consistent user name (e.g. project_firstname). Make sure Skype starts up automatically when starting up your computer, et voila! You have a tailor-made team chat environment that works regardless of where your team members are.

@CTION: If you work in a team or project environment see how you can introduce a chat function. Ask your IT department for possibilities within the current company software, or create your own chat environment for your team with an existing outside solution.

Send less = receive less

Even if you don't believe in the law of attraction, you have probably experienced the following phenomenon: The moment you send out more emails, you receive more emails in the form of questions, replies, remarks and well intended advice.

The same is true for sending out fewer emails. The flow of incoming emails will not dry up completely, but it will get remarkably quieter.

So reducing the flow of outgoing emails is one of the best approaches to reducing the inflow as well. And this is basically a double time saver, since you don't have to write an email that you won't send, and on top of that you won't have to read any of the replies because they won't appear.

A friend of mine shared with me her experience of a situation that showed how difficult it can be to stay true to this principle. "All my colleagues around me were sending and replying to emails on a certain topic. At one point I almost felt obliged to write an email as well, otherwise my boss might think that I was not involved in this project, or even that I didn't care. At that moment I realized how ridiculous that reaction would be, and I didn't send anything."

We discussed the impact of email culture on your own email behavior earlier, didn't we?

When you do need to send an email, you can apply the same 'send less = receive less' principle to the people you put in the Cc field. Even though it seems like one email, in reality you are sending as many email as you've put names in the To and Cc fields. One email with seven people in Cc can easily result in a multitude of emails that you have effectively invited into your inbox.

I know some senior managers who, when they are working in the evening or at night, postpone the sending of their emails to the next morning. This is so they don't disturb their employees in the evening, and it contributes to a healthier email culture. Quite often when they look at their outboxes in the morning, they decide not to send certain emails after all. Receiving less email as a consequence is a fair reward.

@CTION: Put a Post-It note on your desk or screen that says "Do I really need to send this email?" or "Do I really need to put someone in

Cc?" Every email not sent will help you to reduce the flow of incoming emails.

Anticipate questions

Many email responses are to clarify what the sender originally wrote, or to ask additional questions that perpetuate email churn (rather than end a thread succinctly). The easiest way to reduce needless email is to anticipate what your recipient's impressions and questions will be after reading your message, and address any information gaps. If you send a brief email stating, "The budget meeting is canceled today," the reader will probably wonder why, and when the meeting will be rescheduled.

Anticipate the recipient's reaction and communicate more thoroughly, answering questions that you think she'll have. Before hitting Send, slow down to consider: Did I give all the information needed? Will the reader understand my message? Is my point clear? Are the next steps obvious?

Rules or filters are your best friend

Rules or filters play a crucial role in your journey towards spending no more than 15 minutes a day managing your inbox. By using these options that your email client provides, you can automate the process of redirecting emails to their appropriate folders without even seeing them in your inbox. This will have the biggest effect on reducing the flow of emails entering your inbox.

Emails that are part of your job responsibility but don't require immediate action should be directed to a location where you can deal with them at a time you decide is appropriate. For example, let's say you receive a report every month, from the same person with the same subject – you want to read it on the following

Tuesday, so you don't want it hanging around in your inbox. You can set a rule to redirect it to a 'reports to read' folder. And, of course, if there are regular emails that shouldn't be sent to you in the first place, you can filter them to the Deleted or Trash folder.

Rules are very easy to make, and consist of two main parts. The first part is where you define the common characteristics of the emails you want to redirect, so the rule can recognize them every time they arrive in your inbox. These common characteristics could be:

The sender
The subject or part of the subject
The size
The fact that you are in Cc
Words that appear in the body of the text

The second part of the rule is where you define what to do with it:

Send it to a specific folder
Delete it
Mark it with a specific color
Forward it
Automatically reply to it with a specific message

Actually, rules or filters are quite fun to develop, since they give you the feeling that you're outsmarting your inbox. At least that's my experience. And creating rules is something that develops over time. The more you work with *The 15-Minute Inbox* principles, the better you'll become at creating rules.

Example rules

Here are examples of some efficient rules that people have created which helped them to reduce the flow of incoming emails significantly. Use these rules for inspiration and feel free to create new ones that work for you.

Rule: "If file size is larger than 1 MB then send to folder Large Files." The idea behind this rule was that the director in charge noticed that mails with heavy attachments seldom required his immediate action – most of the times these were presentations that he preferred to read only once per day – but they did clog up his inbox and slowed down his server speed.

Rule: "If I am in copy then send to folder CC." This person noticed that emails in which she was copied hardly ever required her immediate action. By redirecting them to her CC folder and quickly checking this folder only four times a day, she saved a lot of time.

Rule: "If the mail is from my manager then color-code it red." Being an assistant, he wanted to follow up quickly on emails from his boss. This rule helped him to create clarity in his full inbox.

Rule: "If email is from [newsletter] then send to folder Read Later." As I mentioned earlier, you want to avoid email entering your inbox that doesn't require your immediate action. Newsletters, quarterly updates and bulletins can be read later today or even tomorrow with a cup of coffee.

@CTION: Go to your inbox and create at least five rules based on the emails you find in your inbox or Trash folder. Here's an easy way to identify if certain types of email qualify for a filter or rule: you can sort them on Sender or Subject to notice any repetitions.

Set email expectations

Establish your email preferences - how often and when you would like to receive them - and make those norms known throughout your company. When leading a project, don't default to being copied on everything. Indicate to your team when you should be copied on emails, and make sure your behavior reflects this.

Likewise, ask your colleagues for their preferences in your communications with them.

Sometimes you may face an important deadline that really requires all your time and attention. At those times, it may help to inform your email community about this by using the out-of-office option.

"Dear sender, this is to let you know that I have received your email. However, I am facing an important deadline that I want to meet. Please don't expect an answer to your email before end of business tomorrow. Thanks for your understanding."

Setting the expectations of when you will respond to emails will definitely reduce the flow of follow-up emails from people expecting a response. (Of course this option doesn't work with every function in an organization. If you need to be accessible for the outside world, you probably don't want to use this. But you get the point.)

Make use of the available productivity tools

You can avoid a lot of email traffic if you use the appropriate tools available. For instance, planning a meeting and trying to align 10 agendas is a nightmare when you have to do it via email. You can imagine the ping-pong that ensues. However, every email client today has a sophisticated calendar function that can be used to plan meetings. Use that instead.

Another tool – or more accurately a habit – to adopt in your organization is to use links instead of sending heavy attachments. Although this will not prevent an email from entering your inbox, it will keep your inbox light and at maximum speed. And, more importantly, if several people are working on a presentation that is stored centrally, you will always get the most updated version when you click on the link. And it will certainly reduce email traffic if you don't have to receive presentation_final.ppt, presentation_final_v2.ppt and presentation_finalfinal.ppt.

@CTION: What can you arrange and communicate to ensure that your team only sends links to heavy documents?

CHAPTER NINE

Treat All and Touch Once: The 4+1 Action Ds

"Trust only movement. Life happens at the level of events, not of words. Trust movement." – Alfred Adler

The power of zero

Each year during summer, my family and I spend a few weeks at a Buddhist monastery in France. One month per year they open the monastery for the public and we get a chance to join their community and experience their way of living. This means we get to start the day with an early morning meditation – a great way to start the day. After each meditation I always feel completely at ease, peaceful, and relaxed. My mind is emptied.

When I clean up my desk in my office (which I am not good at, I have to admit) I feel at ease and in control. It's nice to arrive at my clean desk, and it almost invites me to start working. And I notice that with a clean desk there are far fewer distractions that keep me from doing what I want to do.

When I start cooking I prefer a clean kitchen (which I am not good at, I have to admit) to prepare the meals. The sentence that always comes up is from the Disney Pixar movie *Ratatouille*, where the head chef shouts repeatedly "always keep your work-station clean!"

Looking at these examples, there seems to be something special about 'clean' and 'zero'. I could add a lot of other areas to this list, such as your car, your wardrobe, your kid's bedroom, and your garage, where 'clean' is far preferable to 'messy'.

Mess just doesn't work.

This exact same conclusion is valid for your inbox. You want to have your inbox empty and clean in order to generate the feeling of being in control, at ease, and relaxed. And there is something magic with the number zero. Zero means zero, not one, a few, or 10.

Bringing back your inbox to zero, at least once a day, is the core habit in *The 15-Minute Inbox* process. Let's go for it.

Prepare your terminals

Going back to the concept of your inbox as an airport hub, let's take a look at what structure is needed to move all passengers – or emails –to the correct terminal as fast as possible.

During the day, all kinds of emails arrive in your inbox. This is a process that is out of your control; when an email arrives, you don't know what the content is about, or whether it is addressed to you or if you are just in copy (unless you've set up a rule for that). When they've arrived in your inbox, you want to distinguish the emails that require your action from all the others as quickly as possible. So one terminal – or folder – will be designated to emails that require action. You can call this folder 'action today', 'to do', 'my actions', or any other name that serves this purpose. I will refer to this folder as Action Today.

Another terminal that you want is for emails that need your follow-up; you are either waiting for someone else's input, or you need to check progress on an action. You can compare these to passengers who are in transit – their first flight (action) has been completed, and now they have to wait until they can continue on their journey. So the second folder we create is called 'Follow-up'.

A third terminal that we are going to create is for all emails that don't require your action, but you do need (or want) to read the content. These emails could include interesting newsletters, for-your-info emails, presentations, or relevant articles. For this group of emails we create a folder called 'Read Later'.

@CTION: On top of the folders you already have, create the following three additional folders:

1. *ACTION TODAY*
2. *FOLLOW-UP*
3. *READ LATER*

For the purpose of this process, I suggest to use these exact names – in capitals and including the numbers, so the folders show up neatly underneath each other. As I said, once you master this process, you can fine-tune it to your own system.

The 4+1 Action Ds

The next habit, which is inspired by David Allen's book *Getting Things Done* and Merlin Mann's *Inbox Zero* concept, is crucial in keeping your inbox empty.

Every time you decide to deal with your inbox, treat each email that's in it _only once_. Pick it up out of your hub and drag it to the appropriate terminal by choosing from a limited number of possible actions – five in this case.

Once it is in the right terminal – or folder – you can give it the time and attention it deserves at a time that works best for you.

The 4+1 possible actions you can choose from for each and every email that enters your inbox are the following:

Delete it, or
Deal with it, or
Defer it, or
Delegate it;

and when you're Done, go to the next.

Action D1 – Delete it

Once you've opened your email program, just start from the top and go down the list of new emails. Let's take number one. The first thing you should ask yourself is if you really need this information. Like really. Is it part of your job and are you the right person to deal with it?

If not, before you delete it, think about how you can you avoid receiving it again. If possible, this email, or type of email, should never get into your inbox again. Could you unsubscribe, request to be removed from the mailing list, send a reply that you don't want to be copied on this type of conversation, or create a filter so it will automatically be sent to Trash the next time?

After you have made sure that this email will never get into your inbox again, delete it. Be firm and decisive. Most of the emails you receive should not clutter your inbox.

Now, if you do need the information, and you are the right person to deal with it (don't assume this too easily!), select one of the following options and act accordingly.

Action D2 – Deal with it

If you can deal with a question or request within, let's say, two minutes, just do it immediately. But keep in mind that not every message requires a reply — not even every message that asks a question. Some people are naturally chatty; however, that doesn't mean they'll be offended if you don't respond to every question in every message. (For ways to speed up the reply process, check out the next chapter.)

If you can construct and send a suitable reply within a couple of minutes, do so on the spot and then archive or delete the original message. A lot of questions and information requests can be dealt with quickly. If you have to figure out a reference, telephone number, your availability for a meeting, or this month's market shares, look up the information, check it, copy, paste, done. Don't add a long story to it; provide the data and continue.

When you're done with the message, either archive it (which means put it in either the folder 2. FOLLOW-UP or in its designated folder) or delete it.

Action D3 – Defer it

If a message contains an assignment or implies some action you must take other than merely replying — write an article, look up information, make an appointment — and it may take longer than two minutes, you can choose to defer it (= postpone).

You need to make a decision here. And don't worry, you'll get better with practice. If the activity related to the email will take less than one hour and you need to do it – it is part of your job – move the message into your 1. ACTION TODAY folder. If it will take more than one hour and you need to do it, plan it into your calendar. Don't keep the email in your inbox until you do the task; plan it in and remove the related email from your inbox (folder 2. FOLLOW-UP would be a good place to keep it, right?).

The point of the Action Today folder isn't merely to keep your inbox empty, but to focus your attention on those messages that genuinely require more attention than you can give in a few minutes. So be sure to check your Action Today folder frequently, and move messages out of it (delete or archive) once you've dealt with them. Make it your goal to keep this folder as close to empty as possible. Under no circumstances should you let any message sit there for more than a week. That's why it's called Action Today.

Read only / FYI

Not every message is a top priority. For messages that you may want to look at, but don't really need to spend time on now, use the Read Later folder. In fact, you don't even need to open these emails if you can tell what they are from the sender and subject. Move them straight to your 3. READ LATER folder. Make sure you set up a rule for this message, so you don't have to drag it to this folder yourself in the future. The Monthly Company Update, newsletters you still want to receive or messages starting with FYI fall into this category.

When you have some free time or need a break from your activities, grab a drink and go through your Read Later folder. Don't forget to delete or file the emails you've dealt with as appropriate.

Action D4 – Delegate it

Some messages require action by another person, or they are just not part of your job. In those cases you can delegate the required activity by forwarding the message. Don't forget to include clear instructions (what, by when, how, next action, answer to be sent to, etc.). If you need to follow-up on the progress, file the message in the 2. FOLLOW-UP folder. If you don't need to follow-up, or if you have done already, then delete or archive the email.

Delete it or archive it?

Some messages are clearly worth saving for future reference, but in many cases, it's immediately evident that you'll never need to look at a message again after reading it once. In these cases, I recommend deleting the message right away. If you keep it around, you'll waste time by forcing yourself to re-read it later to determine whether it's important.

And for most information there is a central storage place or source, so if you really need it in the future, you can request a copy or update from someone in a minute. The likelihood is that you'll never need to do that.

Action D5 – Done? Move to the next!

It's important to keep on moving when you're processing your inbox. Don't get distracted by a link, attachment or interesting article. Continue with the next email in your inbox and go through the same process until all of the emails have been dealt with and you have processed your inbox to zero.

Now, of course, it is possible (perhaps very likely) that you will receive new emails while processing your inbox. Decide what you want to do with that. You can keep them (unread!) for processing with the next batch, or include them in the current batch. The most important thing is that you keep moving, deal with one email and go to the next.

The need to complete

Remember, *The 15-Minute Inbox* concept is not only about an empty inbox and the time and attention you put into it. It's about you deciding how much time you want to dedicate to managing your inbox. With some practice, you'll achieve this easily in 15 minutes, but in the beginning it might take a little bit more time.

As we saw earlier, when you complete a task or activity, it is very important to keep the productivity flowing. You are in charge of defining the tasks. This could be, "I will clean up all my emails", or it could be "I will spend 15 minutes cleaning up my inbox now." After 15 minutes you could close your email program, regardless of what is left, and continue with your work. You can see this as a completed task too.

Especially when you're training new habits, working on something like cleaning up your emails in 15-minute pockets is a very effective way of integrating the new habit into your daily behavior. That's the way we try to tackle the continuous mess in our kitchen and living room at home. My kids and I are not really champions when it comes to cleaning up. We pick out everything we need for breakfast, and when we've eaten we only return a plate or cup, leaving most of the breakfast mess on the table. Or when we are cooking, we clean up some of the chopped vegetables and put some plates in the dishwasher, but we still leave a big mess in the kitchen.

So every evening we set a timer for 15 minutes and start cleaning up together. In 15 minutes you can do quite a lot, and the kids love to beat the clock. If they can do it, you can do it.

Inbox 0

And then, after your hard work dealing with all the emails in your inbox, you reach the ultimate goal – the holy grail of email management. Inbox 0. This is an empty inbox with nothing but white space. This is a victorious moment, as it should be. When you reach this point you realize that zero is different than five or 10. Being in control of your inbox seems to be binary; it's either zero or not.

I remember the first time I reached this state of 'inbox 0' – after many years of trying to catch up with the never-ending flow of incoming emails – and it felt like a huge achievement. I don't know what I shouted when I deleted the last email, but I'm sure I shouted something.

It seemed like I had to enjoy it quickly, because before I knew it a new email popped up on my pristine white screen. But, interestingly, I dealt with this email that was disturbing my clean inbox very quickly. I clearly saw it as an intruder of my time, and with a certain amount of pleasure I killed it on the spot.

However, the few days after that felt really strange. It was easy to keep up with the emails coming into my inbox using the 4+1 Action Ds, but the empty inbox made me feel very uncomfortable. I remember checking it more often than I did before, clicking the Send/Receive button to see if there really was nothing coming in, and even checking my internet connection every now and then. I must have looked like a junkie in rehab.

I realized that I couldn't rely on my email anymore to decide what to do today; I was now in charge of my agenda and the priorities I wanted to work on. So it became time to think about that, and I had to smile when I came to that conclusion. Finally, I could be the proactive business builder that I wanted to be.

CHAPTER TEN

Speed Up Your Email Replying and Reading

"In skating over thin ice our safety is in our speed."
– Ralph Waldo Emerson

No speed limits

When dealing with your inbox, there is no limit to how fast you can reply to emails. Actually, speed is a very important ingredient in keeping up with your inbox. Obviously, the faster you can respond to an email that requires an answer, the less time it takes you to deal with the whole list.

But speed goes two ways here. Since you have a huge impact on how fast the recipient of your email can read, understand, and take action on your message, it would only be fair to also optimize the reading speed of the emails you send. And if you believe in reciprocity, you will be rewarded for this behavior in the future with short, crisp and easy to read emails from the people around you.

The speed at which you can reply to an email is influenced

strongly by your capability to typing fast without looking at your keyboard – your touch-typing skill. If you haven't yet mastered this skill, it could be very beneficial to do so. Realizing that the use of keyboards probably won't disappear in the future, our eight-year-old son is now learning to touch type. (I wish I had done that when I was young, it would have saved me a lot of time typing this manuscript!)

In addition to your words-per-minute, which you could call the physical aspect to speeding up your email replies, there is also a mental part. If I receive a full-page email, somewhere in my head that little voice tells me that I just can't answer with one short sentence. Don't listen to that little voice – you can and you should. Too bad for the author of the email novel, he'll just get a brief reply.

Speed up replies

You will benefit greatly from being able to reply quickly – especially to the emails that fall into the category "Deal with it", since they require an action that will take less than two minutes. There are different ways to accomplish this.

First of all, there may be just a short answer to the question that has been asked. Someone wants to know a file number, a phone number, your availability for a meeting, a reference, or a confirmation. Just answer the question, hit send, and delete the email.

In these situations be careful with adding all kinds of unnecessary information like the greeting, the introduction and the closure. The first answer in below example definitely looks much nicer, but in this case it's just taking up precious time. (If you work with people who interpret this as being rude, you can include this in your expectations conversations with your col-

leagues: 'It's faster for me to just reply briefly, so don't be offended if my emails don't include a greeting').

> From: Lucy Goodchild
> To: Joost Wouters
> Subject: Phone number
>
> Hi Joost,
>
> Do you have the phone number of the editor?
>
> Thank you, Lucy.

Answer 1:

> From: Joost Wouters
> To: Lucy Goodchild
> Subject: RE: Phone number
>
> Hi Lucy,
>
> The phone number of the editor is 600210811.
>
> Good luck!
>
> Best regards,
> Joost.

Answer 2:

> From: Joost Wouters
> To: Lucy Goodchild
> Subject: RE: Phone number
>
> 600210811

Another way to reduce the time it takes you to reply, especially
when more than one question is being asked in an email, is to
write your responses in the original message. This also improves
the clarity of your reply and avoids miscommunication. If needed, you can re-arrange the message for even more clarity.

From: Lucy Goodchild
To: Joost Wouters
Subject: Information publisher

Hi Joost,

Could you please help me with the following?

The phone number of the publisher? Address of their office? Two days this week that you can meet with them?

Thanks, Lucy.

Answer:

From: Joost Wouters
To: Lucy Goodchild
Subject: RE: Information publisher

Please find answers in bold below.

-----Original Message-----------

From: Lucy Goodchild
To: Joost Wouters
Subject: Information publisher

Hi Joost,

Could you please help me with the following?

The phone number of the publisher?
678096154

Address of their office?
Church Street, 53
Barcelona

Two days this week that you can meet with them?
Thu & Fri

Thanks, Lucy.

A good way to get yourself into the habit of answering emails with succinct responses is to limit your replies to a maximum of five sentences. After a while you can reduce this to four sentences, and the real diehards can go to three, two or even one sentence.

And really, a long, full-page email doesn't require the same poetical effort from you. If you feel uncomfortable with this, check your beliefs and remember that you are trying to take control of your inbox. (Actually it's also great feedback for the sender if you reply with a quick "okay, good plan" to an overly long email. They should be thinking about their own email habits too.)

Garbage out is garbage in

Do you realize that on average it takes longer to read an email than to write it? Which might seem strange because you'd think reading takes less time than writing.

Well this is technically true, unless you send a long message with an unclear call to action to someone, with five people copied. They all have to spend several minutes deciphering what you mean and what they are supposed to do. And when three of them reply directly to you for more clarification, and the other two do the same, but with a Reply to All, it becomes clear how much time can be wasted because of one unclear email. In this example (which is not far from reality) 21 emails were generated, cluttering seven inboxes, including yours. And it's not over yet.

It might have taken you a couple of minutes to write your initial email. But because of the lack of clarity, the resulting questions and required responses, you ended up spending a lot more time than you needed to on this piece of communication.

In the world of process management, the saying goes "garbage in is garbage out." In the world of inbox management it's the other way around: Garbage out is garbage in.

Example

During an email course that I was facilitating, one of the managers had a revelation. She used to send very long emails because she wanted to be very detailed and correct. In her view, the only way to do this was to be extensive in her communication. She also thought that by explaining everything she was being nice to people. However, she hardly ever got the results or information that she was looking for, and she usually had to wait a couple of days before someone replied.

During the course, her colleagues told her that they never had time to read through her long emails, and so they put her emails lower down in priority. It was like a light bulb switched on. From that moment on she never sent another long email. Now she calls people if she has a question, which saves everyone a lot of time and delivers immediate results.

The P&G one-page memo

One of the greatest skills I learned at Procter & Gamble was to write clear documents. Every employee gets extensive training in the concept that every communication has to fit on one page – with normal fonts and margins – and follow a fixed format. This is a very powerful discipline and it has served me well ever since.

The format was created to serve the reader. The principle idea was that the reader had to go through reams of recommendations all day, so the writer had to arrange the information the way the reader wanted to get it.

1. **The idea:** What is this asking for? What am I, as the reader or approver, being asked to do?

2. **Background:** Remind me of this project, put this in perspective.

3. **How it works:** What is the key benefit/action you are asking for?

4. **Support or reasons why:** A section meant to anticipate and counter the reader's objections.

5. **Next steps:** What's next? When must I approve this by? Who has to do what?

Apart from the service to the reader, this discipline forces the writer to think carefully about the situation at hand and set up a clear structure before sending out a document. If someone returned a memo asking "what about this option?" somewhere in the margin, it signaled that you'd failed in your writing task.

Create clear emails

I wouldn't be surprised if the P&G one-page memo discipline still exists. Either way, the ideas behind this concept can and should be used to create clear emails too. Writing clear and well-structured emails has more than one benefit. It dramatically reduces the processing time for the recipient, it increases the chance that you'll receive the information you're after in one go, and it avoids unnecessary emails in your inbox with clarifying questions.

Most importantly, it helps you in your business thinking. Every email you write is an exercise in clear communication, which you will need outside your inbox as well. And if you know what you want, you will probably include fewer people in the Cc field.

A clear email has certain characteristics. First of all, it has a clear subject. Second, it has a clear structure and layout. And third, it has a clear call to action. Apart from being written without spelling or grammatical errors, in a business-like font and color (I know someone who automatically deletes all emails written in the font Comic Sans, since this is a font for comics, and therefore can't be important), and in a language all recipients (including the ones in copy) can understand.

Clear subject

This is the first hurdle, and the place where most emails go wrong. Subjects like Meeting, Question, Book.xls or Memo, are vague and don't tell you a lot. The subject line should explain what the content of the email is about. Or in other words, there should be a clear correlation between the subject and the content and, if action is required, by when.

Unclear subjects:

Subject: MT Meeting
Subject: New login procedures
Subject: Presentation Brand Review
Subject: Deadline discussion
Subject: CV

Clear subjects:

Subject: Pre-read for MT Meeting June 7
Subject: Login procedures v.5 – Supersedes all previous versions
Subject: Link to Category Presentation – Brand Review Sep 18
Subject: Recommend we ship product May 13th
Subject: CV Candidate KP – Read before interview 10/5 @15:00

In a recipient's full inbox, subject lines are like the titles on a bookshelf. If you want to increase the chance that your email is read, give it a clear subject.

Abbreviations

Sometimes, all that there is to say fits in the subject line. Why waste writing time by copying the same message in the body text or reading time by opening the mail to find no more information? For this situation a commonly used abbreviation is [EOM] or End Of Message.

Subject: MT meeting postponed to Friday Feb 8 @11:00 [EOM]

Another commonly used abbreviation to be used in the subject line is [FYI], or For Your Info, assuming no immediate action is required so the recipient can safely pick a time to take notice of the information and archive it if needed.

Subject: [FYI] Updated Birthday Calendar Sales Department

If you want to pro-actively avoid the flow of incoming email, and you don't need a response from the recipient, in certain situations you can use the abbreviation [NRE], or No Reply Expected.

Subject: Minutes of MT meeting June 7 [NRE]

Of course, if you want to use abbreviations in your email communications, align them first in your team. Otherwise, they only add to the confusion (and they may wonder, "what does he mean with EOM?")

Clear structure and layout

The easiest way to speed up the time it takes the recipient to read an email is to offer a clear structure and layout. Avoid typing everything in one big block of text; instead use paragraphs and white spaces. A clear structure also helps you when scanning your document to see if you've covered everything.

When drafting a substantial email, try to incorporate the structure as explained above in the P&G one-page memo section. It's most important to start with the idea; there's nothing more frustrating for a recipient than to spend time deciphering an email to find out what action they need to take.

Also, don't address more than one topic or question in an email. A golden rule is 'one topic per email', to avoid that the recipients miss a point or gets confused.

If you have one topic with different action steps for the recipients, make this clear as well. When you send an email to more than one person, the required action for each person needs to be clear to everyone. You cannot assume they will find out or decide among themselves.

> *Dear all,*
>
> *This is to confirm our meeting with the Design Team on Thursday April 12. Purpose: To decide on the final product design.*
>
> *Timing: From 12:00 till 13:30, lunch included.*
>
> *Ann -- please forward invitation to meeting participants*
> *Jack -- please book meeting room and catering services*

Watch out for attachments

Depending on compression methods and file format, 1MB of data can roughly be[13]:

- A 1024×1024 pixel bitmap image with 256 colors (8 bpp color depth)
- A 4 megapixel JPEG image with normal compression
- About 1 minute of 128 kbit/s MP3 compressed music

- 6 seconds of uncompressed CD audio
- A typical English book volume in plain text format (500 pages × 2000 characters per page)

Very large mail attachments may be rejected by the recipient's mail server and cause their email inbox to exceed the mail quota; the email with attachment may be bounced back to the sender as 'undeliverable'. Large attachments may also cause the recipient's email to 'hang' when he or she attempts to download the message.

In my experience, something like a 'final' version of a presentation sent by email is likely to be followed up five minutes later by a revised final version and so on. People often notice a mistake they made, or an adjustment that's needed, once they've sent the 'final' version. This can result in three or four attachment-heavy emails in your inbox.

So, a good way to speed up and reduce email traffic is to link to heavy documents, rather than attaching them. Since most teams and organizations work with one or more central drives, this habit should not be too difficult to install. Maybe you need to address this topic in a team meeting and explain (or ask someone else to explain) how it works.

If you don't work with central drives, there are plenty of Cloud services available to store your centrally documents, enabling you to share the link. I use Box.com, Dropbox and iCloud myself, and there are many more out there.

If you write it twice, automate it

A good habit from *The 15-Minute Inbox* is to think about automation whenever you repeat an activity. This includes things that you type often, such as a description of the route to your office, your name, email address, or certain guidelines.

There are several solutions to tackle this. One is to make use of the signature option. You can create more than one signature with information that you need to provide repeatedly.

Another solution is to make use of text expanders. These are programs that enter the full text after typing a shortcut. For example, when I type ".visa", my Visa card number appears, ".e" and my email address pops up and ".jw" transforms into Joost Wouters. (Once you get used to these time saving shortcuts it is very hard to type on someone else's computer!) There are many software solutions on the market, paid and free of charge, but you may have to check with your IT department before you can download a third party solution.

A third solution for automation is to cut and paste blocks of text that you need regularly from a place you can access quickly. A pragmatic solution is to open a new email, enter the blocks of text and save the email as a draft. The subject helps you to locate quickly the text you need (e.g. "Answers Interview Process"), and cutting and pasting is still far faster than rewriting the text time and time again.

CHAPTER ELEVEN

Deal With Your Backlog

"Procrastination is the art of keeping up with yesterday."
– Don Marquis

The backlog approach

By now, you have learned a few effective principles from *The 15-Minute Inbox*. But what should you do with your backlog? What about the remaining 275, 528 or more emails that are still in your inbox?

Good question.

When dealing with backlogs in general, the best approach is to isolate the issue. In this case, create a temporary folder, name it Inbox Backlog - or whatever you like - and drag all the emails in your inbox to the new folder. This only works if you keep your backlog emails in an isolated area; one that doesn't get bigger with new emails coming in.

The benefit is that you have your inbox clean instantly, so you can apply all the new habits from *The 15-Minute Inbox* and see the effects immediately. The risk is that you don't look at the temporary folder any more (out of sight, out of mind), and you may end up facing the consequences. Getting rid of your backlog requires some discipline.

Don't forget that practicing your new email habits and keeping your inbox clean are your biggest priorities. Make sure you empty your inbox to zero at least once a day.

And again, don't add more emails to your isolated Inbox Backlog. It doesn't serve as compensation for any failed email behavior.

Get rid of the backlog

Now that you've isolated and moved your backlog to a separate temporary folder, you probably realize you have to get rid of a substantial number of emails. This is not very motivating.

So, first of all you need to manage your spirit: Don't become demotivated. It is a bold and rewarding journey you are on. Once you succeed, you will have tackled a huge issue, and you can be proud of that while you're still working towards your goal. Make sure your mindset supports you in this battle.

Block time

Make a rough estimation of the time you need for dealing with all the emails in your backlog, and block time slots in your calendar to work on it. Don't try to finish it all in one go. Planning blocks of, for example, 15 minutes each gives you the opportunity to focus your attention on this task in manageable time slots.

Run the rules

The first thing you should do is run all the rules you have created so far. Take advantage of the part of the process that you have already automated and enjoy the effect of messages moving to their designated folders by themselves.

Delete big batches

Now it's time to Delete or Archive big chunks of email. Don't dive into the separate subject lines, but focus on the bigger batches that you can get rid of by sorting on various labels.

Sort on subject

Quickly scroll through the list and delete any batch that has to do with a topic you have already dealt with. Or keep the last message in a conversation and delete the 20 previous emails related to that subject. You can also file a big chunk at once, if you need to keep all the emails.

Sort on sender

Now, sort on sender and scan the batches you can delete or file based on the person who sent the emails. Again, don't go into the specific messages, try to stay on the top level. You're still looking for big chunks to get rid of.

Sort on date

Maybe you can easily delete emails that are older than a certain threshold. Does it really make sense to keep worrying about an email that you haven't dealt with in the last three months? Take a deep breath, select everything older than three months and hit delete. If it was, or is, really important, they will send it again.

Quickly scan emails in which you are copied

Maybe you need to look for it, but most email programs have an option to select or sort emails in which you are copied. This is the group to tackle next. There is probably no action required from you, so quickly scan these messages and act accordingly. In other words, archive or delete.

Treat remaining mail with 4+1 Action Ds

By now, you have probably reduced your backlog by a significant amount. Treat the remaining messages with the 4+1 Action Ds. Start at the top of the list and then either:

- Delete it (check if you can set up a rule before deleting to avoid receiving this message again in the future)
- Deal with it (if less than two minutes), and delete or file afterwards
- Defer it (put in 1. ACTION TODAY, 3. READ LATER or plan in agenda and then 2. FOLLOW-UP)
- Delegate it (and delete or in 2. FOLLOW-UP)
- And when you are done with it, move to the next.

Set a timer and process quickly

The key to successfully eliminating your backlog is in the pace of processing. You should dedicate limited time slots of, let's say, 15-minute blocks to this task. Use the timer function on your phone or tablet and set it to 15 minutes. Stop as soon as the alarm goes off.

During these 15 minutes, you process more quickly and purposefully, with concentration. Don't end up reading into an email and get distracted. Catch yourself if this happens and get back to the task again.

Process all your emails, down to zero. That's your mission. And once your backlog session is complete, close the temporary Inbox Backlog folder and continue with your day. Tomorrow or later today you can continue with the next batch. Processing those batches really adds up, and before you know it you will have gone through your whole backlog.

Email bankruptcy is not the solution

Some people declare themselves email bankrupt. In a last hopeless effort to manage their email overload, they delete all their emails and start again with a clean sheet. This seems like a quick and easy solution, but unfortunately it's only a false illusion that things will become better.

If you don't change some critical email behavior, you will end up with a huge backlog again in no time. You need to find structural solutions for dealing with your email overload. There is no such thing as a free lunch.

That's basically all there is to say about dealing with your backlog. In the end, it's your backlog to deal with, and you have to do it yourself. Pull up your sleeves and go for it!

CHAPTER TWELVE

Create a Crystal Clear Archiving Architecture

"Do not dismantle the house, but look at each brick, and replace those which appear to be broken, which no longer support the structure."
– Neale Donald Walsch

Why do you file?

Why do you file and store messages? The only valid answer would be that you need the emails you keep for future reference. Now, if you look at your current folders and the emails contained in them, I'm positive that you have never looked at most of the emails since they were filed. At least 80% of the messages that are stored in your folders are collecting digital dust.

The main reason we drag messages into one of the folders on the left panel of our email programs is the same reason our bookshelves are overflowing (even though you hardly ever read a book twice), your clothes closet is exploding (even though you'll never wear those shirts any more) or why your garage or attic is stuffed with things (even though you don't need that old cooking set).

Why? Because you never know! Maybe one day...

Filing means easy placement of — and access to — information. Within *The 15-Minute Inbox* concept we look at all aspects of email that take away time or attention from what we really want or need to do. If you decide to keep most of your emails, make sure you optimize this part of email management. Remember you lose time with the decision to file or delete it, with the decision of where to file it, with finding the correct folder and with retrieving the email if you need it again.

All of these seconds add up.

Peace of mind filing

So it is OK to file. If you don't yet feel confident enough to delete more than you archive, that's fine. Let's call it Peace of Mind filing. But don't use it as an excuse to file everything or to lose a lot of time with an inefficient filing structure. It would still be very valuable to practice the art of deleting, and aim for a better Delete vs. Archive ratio over time.

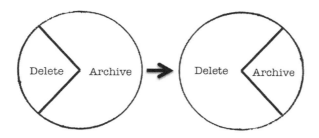

To grow your Delete vs. Archive ratio and minimize the time you need to find the right folder, you have to face and overcome the following two filing fears:

1. Afraid to make a decision
2. Afraid to throw something away

If you are afraid to make a decision and you don't know what category a message falls into or what to call it, you will end up calling it nothing. And if it doesn't have a name, it doesn't get a home. This indecision probably prevents you from deleting the email, because you don't know what you're deleting.

If you are afraid to throw anything away, and you feel like you never know if you might need it one day, then decide against filing. We have discussed this already. Only file a message if there is a reasonable chance you will need it for future reference. Don't file everything.

The biggest decision fear-facing experience of my life was when my wife challenged me years ago to throw away all our books. She didn't like the walls covered with hundreds of different books of varying colors and sizes, and she thought it was a waste of space.

For me, that was something I couldn't even consider. My books. You don't throw away books. You keep books on a bookshelf. You buy more bookshelves if you run out of space. You put them nicely in order by author name or category.

But I never read books twice. I had maybe 10 books that I used for reference every now and then, but the rest remained untouched on the shelf, collecting dust. Proving to the world how literate I was.

I can't remember why, but one day I agreed. I picked out the 10 books I still needed for work and we packed all the rest in cases and took them to a book dump. We went for dinner with the money we got back.

We still buy books, of course. But after reading them, we give them away.

Eliminate filing time wasters

You don't have to file it. The fastest way to save time on filing is to not file at all, and delete the message. Before you decide to archive something, ask yourself the following questions:

Does the message relate to a meaningful objective you're currently working on? If not, you can probably delete it. Why keep information that doesn't relate to your main focus?

Does the message contain information you can find elsewhere? If so, delete it.

Does the message contain information that you will refer to within the next six months? If not, delete it.

Does the message contain information that you're required to keep? If not, delete it.

Another time waster is the way your archive is structured and the time it takes you to find the right folder when filing or retrieving a message. Don't create all your folders on the top level; you don't want Clients, Company Updates, Holidays, Private, and Projects all mixed up just because your email program sorts them in alphabetical order. Instead, create clear names for top-layer folders, ideally written in capitals so they jump out. Then use relevant folder names for the sub folders.

Don't use abbreviations or create names that you'll probably forget in the future. For instance, you may wonder "what did I put in Private1 and what went in Private2?"

And finally, make sure your archive is visually attractive. If your folder list looks like a fragmented, chaotic mess, with some folder names starting with capitals, and some not, you get distracted every time you try to file or retrieve a message. A visually well-structured archive will help you to minimize the time you spend on it.

What is the right filing structure?

The opportunity to file your emails plays an important role in keeping your inbox empty. In this case, out of sight, out of mind is something that you want to realize.

I have seen archiving structures that were extremely detailed, going four to five levels deep, with a total of over 300 folders. You can imagine how much time you waste locating the right folder. Even if this means only a few seconds each time, those seconds add up. The same time is lost (or even more), if you need to retrieve the message. Once you have all your folder layers open, it becomes a visual blur, and you lose precious time locating the right folder.

At the other end of the spectrum, I have worked with people who had only two folders: Received and Sent. They didn't lose any time locating the right folder when filing. They put everything in the Received folder. They realized that they probably wouldn't need to retrieve messages, and, if they did, it would only take a fraction of a minute to search for a specific message. This can be done by sorting by name or topic, or by searching for key words.

For most of us, the reality is probably somewhere in between. I do have five top-line folders, written in capital letters, that represent the most important activities I'm working on right now. Underneath those, I have sub folders where relevant. For instance underneath my top-line folder PROJECTS, I have sub folders for my clients such as Heineken, Imperial Tobacco, Nestlé, Reckitt Benckiser, Sara Lee, and Unilever. Underneath Reckitt Benckiser I have sub folders for the different countries I work with, such as Belgium, Germany, Netherlands, Nordics, Switzerland, and Turkey. For me, that's the maximum: three levels deep.

If I have all my top-line folders closed, my archive looks nice, neat and peaceful.

How to set up your filing

First of all, take a piece of paper. You have to make your structure visual.

An effective archive represents the projects, topics and activities that you are working on. If you were to show me your folders, it should be clear to me what your main responsibilities are and what key projects you are working on. I call these the main buckets.

Step one is to define the main buckets. What are your job responsibilities? Try to look at the bigger picture.

If you are a manager, the folder TEAM should probably be in your list, with team members, team meetings, succession planning, and other team related folders underneath. If you are a marketing manager, the different brands you are responsible for should probably be top-line folders. If you work with clients, internal or external, or projects, you should create a top-line folder named PROJECTS or CUSTOMERS. If you have four main areas of responsibility, AREA 1, AREA 2, AREA 3 and AREA 4 should be top-line folders. Of course you can use your own names.

Since you will most likely receive personal messages too, the folder PRIVATE could make the list. And PERSONAL DEVELOPMENT could serve for all your training, appraisals, salary updates, development plans and holiday information.

Use the top-line folders only to indicate the main buckets, avoid storing email directly here. And try to minimize the number of buckets.

On top of your folder list, you have the three folders that we discussed earlier and that you need to quickly allocate messages when processing your email:

1. ACTION TODAY
2. FOLLOW-UP
3. READ LATER

In these three folders you do store messages directly underneath.

@CTION: Take a blank piece of paper and create a logical top-line archiving structure from scratch. Not from what you have right now. Then implement it and drag the folders that you have right now underneath them. Don't change all the current folder names, you don't want to confuse yourself too much in this phase. You can optimize the folders within one bucket later if you want.

Keep your archive dynamic

Your archive is a dynamic structure, not a static one. You want to have your filing structure quickly and easy accessible for the relevant folders. And relevance changes over time.

Project folders containing emails related to an initiative you are working on right now might become less important a year from now, when the initiative has been launched. When you move to another department, many folders you needed in your previous function may become irrelevant. Team members change or move, so the folders with their names probably don't have to stay in your archiving structure.

I constantly keep my filing system up to date. The best way to do so is to block half an hour in your agenda each month on Filing Maintenance. Remember, if you don't block this time, the idea will die as a nice intention.

In this half hour, I only go through my folder structure and see where I can optimize it to support my current projects and activities. What folders should I move? Is the name of the folder still accurate? What folders can I collapse, and which ones can I delete?

Don't go into the level of the emails that are in each folder to select the messages that could be deleted! This will be a huge distraction and before you know you have wasted an hour without having achieved anything. Deleting 50 or even 100 emails does not have a big impact on the thousands of emails that are probably stored in your archive.

Stay on the folder level and delete or move complete folders if needed, not the separate emails in them.

@CTION: Block monthly half hour slots, or more if you want, in your agenda for Filing Maintenance. Why not every last Friday of the month?

Step 3:

I is for Implementation and Integration

In the previous section, Actions and Automation, you learned what to do to manage your daily email inflow and bring your inbox down to zero. In this section, we will look at how you can integrate these action steps and new behavior into your daily habits, enabling you to maintain this state of control over your inbox permanently.

In this M.A.I.L. step, you will find all the support needed to implement the new habits that will serve you in controlling your inbox, and to integrate them in your daily behavior.

The last chapter of the Implementation and Integration step will deal with situations when email goes wrong. When should you not use email? How can you deal with an email that upsets you? And what can to do when an email ends up in a disaster?

CHAPTER THIRTEEN

Create New Email Habits

"Motivation is what gets you started. Habit is what keeps you going."
– Jim Ryun

What is a habit?

Human beings are creatures of habit; they do things or they don't do things. Your actions, your responses, the decisions you make, and the way you live your life are all largely dictated by your habits.

So what is a habit[14]? In simple terms, it is a behavior or a set of behaviors that you do automatically, without thinking or consciously intending. You automatically put on your seatbelt when you get in your car: that's a habit. You find yourself biting your fingernails: that's a habit. You quickly check your email before going to sleep: that's a habit.

According to Wikipedia:

Habits are automatic routines of behavior that are repeated regularly, without thinking. They are learned, not instinctive, human behavior that occurs automatically, without the explicit contemporaneous intention of the person.

Just as we have supportive habits, we also have non-supportive habits: habits that are negative or unproductive, such as checking your emails every five minutes. You could say that a habit is supportive or successful if it enables you to reach your goal faster and easier.

There are no good or bad habits, just some habits that support you in what you want to realize and some that don't. And it is possible that what once seemed to be a supportive habit, like immediately checking your email when it came in (10 years ago when you received two emails a day) is not as supportive anymore (now that you receive 150 emails a day). Just like not talking to strangers was a habit that served you well when you were three years old, but not anymore now you're 35.

Habit formation

In essence, our habits are a series of patterns[15]. When you first put on your socks, then your shoes, then tie your shoelaces, that whole process is an example of a pattern. Whenever we perform these patterns, our nerve cells take messages back to the brain about the patterns. In this way, a physical neural connection is created. This neural connection allows us to quickly re-access that set of behavior, actions or feelings. This explains why something seems to get easier and more natural the more we do it. The purpose of these neural connections is to make routine tasks easier and faster. The more frequently you do something, the bigger and stronger the neural connection becomes.

By now, the patterns you have created with regards to the way you deal with emails and your inbox are probably well ingrained. You enter your office, grab a cup of coffee, open your laptop, and dive into your inbox. Or when you have your weekly team meeting, you keep your smart phone or laptop at hand to check each new email that comes in. Or you may brush your teeth, set the alarm on your phone, and quickly check your emails. These habits are all supported by neural connections.

The good news is that just as a neural connection can become bigger and stronger when you do something often, it can also become smaller and weaker if you stop yourself from doing it. The connections act like muscles: The more you use them, the bigger and stronger they get. The less you use them, the weaker and smaller they becomes.

How long does it take to change habits?

It depends. There is a common concept that it takes 21 days to change a habit. However, according to a recent study[16], a daily action like eating fruit at lunch or running for 15 minutes took an average of 66 days to become as much of a habit as it could be. Most importantly, there was a lot of variation, both among people and among habits – some people are more habit-resistant than others, and some habits are harder to pick up than others.

The same goes for those who have implemented the new habits from *The 15-Minute Inbox*. My personal experience is that it took only a few days to clean up my inbox and get rid of the huge backlog, and I have even seen people do it in just a couple of hours. However, it can take several months to fully integrate the corresponding habits to keep it like that.

Today, almost three years later, I still have my inbox empty at least once every day, and I am still optimizing my email management by deleting more instead of filing, installing new rules and opting out from unwanted newsletters and notifications. This constant optimization is for me the clear evidence that I have changed my email habits.

All new habits from *The 15-Minute Inbox*

If we put together all *The 15-Minute Inbox* habits that you want or need to master in order to become a master of your inbox, you have to agree that it is not a huge list:

The Five 15-Minute Inbox Habits:

1. Deal with email in batches, during limited, fixed times every day
2. Process your inbox to zero at least once a day
3. Constantly create filters, opt-out and delete faster
4. Think before you send
5. Plan filing maintenance once a month

What you will notice is that for some habits you have another, maybe conflicting habit that you need to change. You can process your email to zero instead of leaving it in your inbox. Others, like creating filters might be new habits that you just need to add to your current email routines.

The process of changing a habit

Let's start with the most difficult ones, the email habits that you need to change. If you want to reduce the time you spend managing your emails, you need to change some of your existing habits, as they are likely to be counter-productive.

Changing a habit is one of the most challenging tasks that a person can undertake. I'm sure you have plenty of examples based on personal experience that prove this statement. In the past, I have tried to run every day, wash the car every week, and clean up the kitchen after cooking, and none of these habits have made it into a strong neural connection.

Luckily, I also have some examples of habits I did successfully change or add to my routines. For instance, flossing my teeth is now something I do without thinking, whereas 10 years ago it was a concept my dentist could only dream about. Twice or three times a week you can find me on my spinning bike, something I've managed to do every week for the past three years.

Often the difficulty in changing your habits has nothing to do with ignorance or attitude. Most people know intellectually when certain habits don't support them and are destructive, not only to themselves but also to the people around them. They genuinely want to change but are just unable to do so.

Unfortunately, willpower alone will probably not be enough to help you change a habit. Relying on willpower may end up in a struggle, with minimal chances of success. For example, my intentions to run every day or clean my car weekly failed as habits supported by willpower alone.

Instead, here is a process to help you change a habit successfully. It follows the H.A.B.I.T. acronym, which stands for:

H - Have a look at your beliefs.

A - Accountability! Own it, don't blame others, and take accountability for the situation.

B - Benefits and Costs? Be aware of the benefits and the price you pay for your current habit.

I - Instead? Choose a new habit.

T - The future? What are the results of the new habit?

H) Have a look at your beliefs

As we saw in the section Mirrors and Mindsets, you will find a belief at the base of each habit. The habits you have developed are a perfect match for these beliefs, and almost prove the beliefs. So, if you don't change your underlying beliefs, it will be very difficult to change your habits.

Let's have a look at the first two *15-Minute Inbox* habits:

15-Minute Inbox - Habit 1:
Deal with email in batches, during limited, fixed times every day

15-Minute Inbox - Habit 2:
Process your inbox to zero at least once a day

What do you currently believe about these habits? Why would they be impossible for you to implement?

I receive too much email every day.

It's impossible to manage so many emails in a day.

In my function I need to be in contact with many people.

_____

_____

_____

_____

These are your underlying non-supporting beliefs.

Now, what habits did you create to prove these beliefs?

I check my email immediately in the morning.

I bring my laptop to meetings to check email in between topics.

I have my email program always running on the background.

_____

_____

_____

_____

A) Accept full accountability for this situation

If you want to change any habit, you need to take full responsibility for your life. You cannot blame anyone else for your situation. If you do, you take yourself out of control.

This might be convenient, because if you can blame others you don't have to take action. But it won't help you achieve what you want. There is only one person who can change your life and your habits, and that is you.

So if you want to build successful email habits, you need to make a declaration to yourself:

"I am 100% responsible for my inbox. It is my life, my time and my attention. I decide how and where to spend it. And even if I don't know how yet, I will find a solution to manage my daily email flow."

If you don't want to stand up from behind your desk and declare this out loud, at least read it three more times.

B) Benefits and costs of your current habits

Every habit has benefits and costs. Your current habits have a function, even if you know changing them would be better. For example, take the habit of smoking. Many people smoke when they feel nervous or stressed. To them, smoking is actually an outlet to reduce their nervousness and anxiety. So that is the function that brought the habit into being.

As long as the costs don't outweigh the benefits, you will probably keep them. So, it is important to realize what would happen if you didn't change your current habits. What are the costs and the benefits?

What are the benefits of these habits?

Convenient, not having to take responsibility.

Avoiding doing boring tasks.

Keep me in action mode, gives adrenalin.

Show how busy (important) I am.

Proving that I have a tough job.

_____

_____

_____

_____

What is the price you might pay if you don't change your current email habits?

Stress, being overwhelmed and always in reactive mode.

Relationship with my family (if I'm behind my laptop all evening).

A lot of additional work.

Bad example for my team members.

No time to create winning strategies that really move our business forward.

_____

_____

_____

_____

Have a look at both lists. Are the benefits bigger than the costs? Or are the costs outweighing the benefits? Have an honest look at the price you might pay if you keep your current email habits alive, and come up with some alternatives. If you feel comfortable with the current situation there is no motivation to change.

I) Instead choose new habits that support you

If you don't find something else to fulfill the function of your current habit, eventually you will have to go back to the old habit because the need isn't being met. Take the above example; if smokers do not find an alternative outlet to release their nervousness and anxiety, such as exercising, meditating or taking up a hobby, they will eventually go back to the habit of smoking.

Our greatest gift in life is that we have free will. Every second you have an opportunity to make a different choice. To do or not to do; to let go or to hold on; to take the easy or the difficult route; to change it or keep it as it is.

What email habits could you choose instead of your existing, non-supportive ones that will support you in becoming a master of your inbox?

Doing my email in batches at limited, fixed times per day.

Processing my inbox to zero at least once per day.

_____

_____

_____

_____

T) The future? How will your life look with these new habits?

You must have strong, clear reasons for wanting to change a habit. Your desire for changing a habit can be to gain something, to help achieve success, to improve yourself or to prevent something from happening. Your reasons should include the results of this change – how it will specifically impact your life (and the lives of those around you).

This is a very important step. When you don't have strong reasons for changing a habit, it is very easy to lose drive and determination. You have nothing to fall back on. Like I said, changing a habit is a tough task, and you'll definitely face difficulties and discomfort along the way. If you don't have strong reasons for changing a habit, you'll be more likely to give up trying.

What makes a professional sprinter train for eight hours a day?

What makes him go through all the pain and discomfort of the training? Is he likely to train as hard if there are no Olympics or World Championships? Definitely not!

Give yourself strong reasons for changing a habit.

What are the results of adapting the new habits?

_____

_____

_____

_____

_____

_____

Celebrate success and be kind to yourself

Congratulations!

Now you have chosen your new email habits, it's time to create a support structure to practice and get used to them. In the next chapter, we will look into specific actions you can take to make the change in habits actually happen.

Remember that your old habits are patterns ingrained in your neural system. It is not that they will disappear the moment you say so, and it is very likely that they'll pop up every now and then. Don't let them put you down.

If you didn't manage it today, start over again tomorrow. Don't punish yourself. If you planned to spend 15 minutes yesterday cleaning up your email backlog and you failed to do so, don't force yourself to do 30 minutes today; 15 minutes a day is 15 minutes a day.

In the same way, celebrate your successes and reward yourself for your accomplishments, big or small. Celebrating success is food for continuation and growth.

CHAPTER FOURTEEN

Fall Seven Times, Stand Up Eight

"Fall seven times, stand up eight." – *Japanese Proverb*

Get in line and stay in line

Have you ever been at a very busy airport with a huge queue to get through security? If your goal is to catch your plane, you know you have to pass through security; there is no way around it. I remember once in Chicago where I found myself, already slightly late, at the back of a long queue. I could see the line meandering in front of me and I counted at least 15 turns before mine. This was going to take ages. I checked the barrier that was separating the flock to see if there was a way to shortcut the line unnoticed, but I didn't have the guts to go through with it.

I had to wait in line until I reached the x-ray machine, where I was summoned to strip my outer layers and put all my electronics and liquids in a tray. If I had stepped out of the queue before I'd reached the x-ray machine, for whatever reason, I would have had to start over again at the end of the line.

The same goes for integrating your new email habits into your daily behavior. It will take some time, and there isn't a shortcut you can take; it will require practice and discipline. There will be days where you'll succeed and days where you won't, but eventually you will get there. And don't forget: if you step out of the line before you have changed your old non-supportive habits for new supportive ones, you'll be back to square one.

Make sure you don't forget

This may sound obvious, but the biggest reason many great plans and ideas don't get implemented is that we forget about them. It is not a lack of intention or incapacity, just memory.

So the very first step you should take after choosing your new habits is to set up a structure to keep you in line. You can have all the best intentions in the world, but you still need a structure that will support you in breaking your old patterns, helping you take the time to practice your new habits so you don't forget about them. The airport in Chicago used barriers to keep me in line; a structure that helped me to get from the end of the queue to the x-ray machine at security. The barriers reminded me to stay in line.

What tools do you currently use to remember things? Here are some tools that can help you create good email habits.

The 30-Day Reminder Service

I have created a unique tool to help you to remember: The "30-Day Reminder Service." If you sign up, you will receive a daily reminder for the next 30 days with a useful tip to keep you in line. And yes, you will receive this reminder by email.

If you go to www.15MinuteInbox.com/30Days, you can get started just by submitting your name and email address. The service is free of charge, exclusively for readers of this book.

Set up your Action Today, Read Later, and Follow-Up folders

At this stage, I recommend that you carry out one of the actions suggested in the section Actions and Automation: set up your Action Today, Read Later, and Follow-Up folders. Once you become more familiar with the *15-Minute Inbox* principles, you can adjust them to your own needs. The most important thing is that you set up a structure that enables you to redirect your emails away from your inbox.

@CTION: If you haven't done so yet, implement the steps suggested in Actions and Automation. Make sure you have the three additional folders as a structure for dealing with all the emails that arrive in your inbox.

Calendar and agenda

@CTION: If you need to get rid of your backlog, block realistic time slots in your calendar to deal with it. For example, plan a 15-minute slot on each day this week to clear your backlog.

@CTION: If you want to limit your email management to certain times of the day, block the time in your calendar. For example, you could plan four slots of 15 minutes to start with. You can always reduce the time later.

Post-It notes on your screen

Make your intentions and new habits visible. It helps if you can see a reminder, just like a shopping list. Set small, daily goals that will help you integrate the new habits. You could put a Post-It note on your computer that says "Install 3 new rules today." Or "Resist the urge to check!"

Create a password for a new habit

Somebody once suggested that if you create a computer password that reflects the habits you want to install, you will be reminded of them more often. By typing the password repeatedly, you will force yourself to integrate the habits. Passwords such as "ilikeinbox0", "15minuteinbox", or "4+1actionDs" can help you focus on eliminating excess inbox messages.

Involve others: ask for their support

Make your partner, assistant, colleague or kids part of your *The 15-Minute Inbox* journey: they will love to help you remember your new habits. My 12-year-old son looks over my shoulder every now and then, and one of his favorite remarks is "Hey Mr. 15-Minute Inbox, I see 12 emails!"

It helps a lot if you're not alone on this journey. In the next section – Leverage and Liberation – you will experience the power of leveraging *The 15-Minute Inbox* principles in your team or department.

Integrate new habits in existing routines

As we saw in the previous chapter, habits are underpinned by patterns. What existing patterns or routines do you currently have, that you could use as a foundation for a new habit? It's much easier if you can link a new email habit to your established routines. Or maybe there's a routine you can adjust slightly so it will help you master your inbox.

I once worked with a management assistant who wanted to start a new habit, so she started by exploring her morning routine. First she would grab a coffee, then open up her computer and start working on emails. She wouldn't stop for the rest of the day. She never made a distinction between processing her inbox and actually dealing with and following up on emails.

We discovered that it would make a big difference if she first processed her emails by sending them to relevant folders (like the ones you have created), before starting her actual work, which was to follow up on some of the emails. How did her existing routine support this? With just one small change: she now drinks her coffee in between the "processing time" and "working time", in order to clearly mark the difference between the tasks. And the promise of coffee gives her an extra stimulus to finish the processing quickly.

@CTION: *Explore your daily routines (arriving at the office, going for lunch, getting a coffee, returning from a meeting, etc.) and see where and how you can use or adjust your routines to integrate your new supportive email habits.*

Play the game

If I look back at the times I really wanted to accomplish something, such as selling a certain number of training programs, earning a specific amount of money or having my inbox empty for a certain number of days in a row, I always made a game out of it. How does this work?

The first step is to make your goal specific and quantifiable – for example, you want to have an empty inbox for 30 days in a row. Then you make this goal visible by dividing it into the number of units you're using to measure your success (in this case, 30 days). Then you need to visualize it: on a piece of paper, draw thirty things that represent the days – this could be smileys, envelopes, squares, or whatever works for you. And then you can keep track of the progress you're making, day by day.

An interesting thing to observe is that gaps tend to be filled. If there is a pothole in the road, fills up with mud, sand and leaves. An empty spot on a bookshelf will be filled in no time at all. And the same goes for the 'gaps' you use to symbolize the journey towards achieving your goal. The more ticks you can put in those circles that represent each day, the more committed you will be to complete the rest. And you can make the rules even stricter by saying that you have to start from scratch if you miss a day.

To make this work, you need to enjoy it: this should be a game. Don't take it too seriously. In my courses, I usually distribute a sheet with 100 envelopes, so people can tick off each successful "Inbox 0 Day" for the next three months. Download your own Play the Game Sheet at www.15MinuteInbox.com/Downloads.

One habit at a time

There is another obstacle that may arise when you're attempting to change your habits: your inner perfectionist. You should not aim for perfection all the time. It's all about progression, not perfection. Taking smaller steps will lead you to greater results in the future. If you start by focusing on one new daily habit rather than tackling your whole approach to email at once, you will have a better chance of successfully integrating that habit into your routine.

The Five *15-Minute Inbox* habits:

1. Check your emails at limited and fixed times each day. Change your email settings so that your email program only checks the server for new messages every hour. By doing this, you will be able to get your work done undisturbed (by incoming emails, at least).

Trust me, breaking this habit takes time. Don't get frustrated when you're constantly clicking the "Send/Receive" button to check for new emails before the hour is up. If you feel the urge to check, you can use a timer to tell you when you're allowed to process your emails again. You can remove temptation by closing your email program after your processing timeslot is finished. And remember: you don't need to open your email program automatically when you start work in the morning. Why not work on something that really needs to be done instead?

2. Process your inbox to zero at least once a day. Start working on it and invest time in this habit: it will pay out dramatically! If you can't process your inbox to zero every time you work on it, then at least clean it up once every day. By mastering this step, you will be assured that, regardless of how many emails you receive, you will be able to process them all each day. The timer could come in handy here too, to help you limit yourself to 15 minutes each time you process your emails.

3. Constantly create filters, opt-out, and delete faster. The default habit here is to delete a message, but at the start you'll want to stop for a moment and take the time to opt-out, or create a rule if applicable. This will reduce the number of emails you need to delete in the future. If you forget to unsubscribe or create a filter when an email first appears, you can always go to your Trash folder and look for emails you can block from now on.

4. Think before you send. Count to three before you hit Send. Is this email the most effective means of communicating right now, or are you just being lazy? If you become more aware of what you send out, you will send fewer emails over time. Don't contribute to the game of email ping-pong by bouncing an email back as quickly as possible without actually solving anything.

5. Plan for filing maintenance once a month. This is a relatively easy one, at least when it comes to planning in half an hour each month for maintenance. Actually doing the work regularly will be more of a challenge. Two incentives: keep your archive dynamic, and give yourself a nice reward if you have done the work.

Be aware of procrastination

Procrastination refers to the act of replacing high-priority actions with those of lower priority, or putting off important tasks so you can do something from which you derive enjoyment.

Procrastination may result in stress, a sense of guilt and crisis, severe loss of personal productivity, or social disapproval for not meeting responsibilities or commitments. These feelings combined may even cause further procrastination.

If you're honest with yourself, you probably know when you're procrastinating. But just in case, here are some useful indicators that will help you identify your own procrastination:

- Being busy with being busy. Filling your day with low priority tasks from your action list.
- Going to your inbox to see if new emails have arrived.
- Sitting down to start a high-priority task, and almost immediately going off to make a cup of coffee (one of my favorites).
- Leaving an item on your action list for a long time, even though you know it's important.
- Regularly saying "Yes" to unimportant tasks that others ask you to do, and filling your time with these instead of getting on with the important stuff that really makes a difference in your job.
- Waiting for the "right mood" or the "right time" to tackle the important task at hand.

When you catch yourself procrastinating, face it and get over it. In Chapter Eighteen, I will present the ultimate time management system. One of the elements of the system is to plan the most confronting task for that day as the first thing you do. Once you have overcome your main obstacle, the rest of the day will flow easily.

Create a compelling future

During a race, athletes often use the push-and-pull effect to help them run as fast as possible. The competitor running next to you pushes you forwards, while the finish line – with all its prizes and promises of fame – pulls you in the same direction. So there are two forces acting together to get you to the finish line as quickly as possible.

The same logic applies to successfully changing a habit. You need to have a push and a pull – a stick and a carrot. And if the carrot is really nice and juicy, you have even more of a reason to achieve your goal.

What would you do with an extra hour each day? How would you spend it? Would you spend it on your business, on yourself, on the opportunity to learn something new, or to improve your relationships with your team members?

Make sure you create a compelling and attractive future for your new situation – one that is worth fighting for.

What would you do with an extra hour each day?

_____

_____

_____

_____

And what would be the result of an empty inbox each day? More time, money, or peace of mind? Feeling good about being in control? What would be possible with an empty inbox that isn't possible now?

What could an empty inbox result in?

_____

_____

_____

_____

Anticipate failure

When you're doing something new, you have to become comfortable with failure. That might sound a bit strange, but since success is the opposite of failure, you need to be able to cope with both before you can really enjoy success.

If you can't get comfortable with failure, you will be set back immediately when something doesn't work out exactly the way you had planned. Failure will happen. You will get distracted, forget, or fall back into old behavior. If you miss a day here or there when you're trying to develop the new habits, it doesn't derail the whole process, so don't get discouraged if you can't keep a perfect track record.

One piece of advice, though: the first few days seem to make the biggest difference, so it's worth trying to be particularly diligent at the beginning of your habit acquisition attempt.

Anticipate success

I remember that when my inbox was empty for three days in a row, something strange happened. I was sitting behind my computer screen and checking my inbox every minute. If it was empty, I was hitting the 'Send/Receive' button to see if new mail was waiting. (You never know – I had changed my settings to check the server once every hour, so I could have missed a new email). And I felt strange, almost a bit lost.

It was obvious to me that now I had achieved my goal, I needed to get used to a new world – one in which it was me in charge, not my inbox. I needed to decide what to do, rather than just replying to an email. I could finally be the proactive business builder I wanted to be. And, to be honest, I hadn't expected it to feel so unreal.

Many people share this experience when they achieve an empty inbox. So if you're sharing this feeling, and just itching to check for new emails, do what I did: Laugh about it and give yourself a huge congratulations for your achievement!

CHAPTER FIFTEEN

When Email Goes Wrong

"If things go wrong, don't go with them." – *Roger Babson*

Explosive email

Sometimes, emails can lead to explosions. When you return from a two-week holiday, your inbox has exploded. When you receive an email that really upsets you, it feels like a bomb has gone off in your inbox. And if you send an email to someone to vent your anger, you could have sent a hand grenade with it.

Accidentally hitting 'Reply All' and sending a private message meant for only one or two people to a huge list is the stuff of nightmares. And the 'Forward' button gives us another good reason to keep a clean inbox – many an explosion has gone off after that's been hit (especially in cases where sensitive information has gone public – even to the press).

In this chapter, we will discuss the explosive sides of email.

The five step back-from-holiday backlog buster

I am sure you have experienced this. Coming back from a nice, relaxing holiday you almost dread the return to your office. You know what's coming: An exploded inbox and the knowledge that you're holiday vibes will melt away in just a few hours among all the things that happened while you were away.

There is another way: one that will cost less energy and protect your holiday vibes.

First of all, don't be surprised that you have a full inbox. This is not the first time you've come back from a holiday, or a two-day training course, or even just a long meeting. You know you'll have a lot of emails in your inbox. Don't complain; instead, act proactively and get rid of your backlog as soon as possible.

Step 1. The first thing you do – before you go on holiday – is block some time immediately after your holiday to deal with your backlog. If you set an Out of Office responder and you include the period you're not accessible in your message, add one day to your holiday; this will give you time to deal with your post-holiday backlog. Make sure you block a few hours – either the whole morning or three blocks of one hour – on your first day back. This will prevent other people from claiming your time for their meetings.

Step 2. Use the first 15 minutes of your block to scan your inbox and delete big batches of emails. Sort by Sender and go through the list quickly, deleting or archiving blocks of emails where appropriate. Then sort by Subject and do the same. Finally, sort by Date and see if you can delete the oldest (and therefore least relevant) emails.

Don't fully read or respond to any emails at this stage.

Step 3. Keep up the speed. You're still trying to get rid of the most obviously irrelevant emails, so you should scan quickly, decide and delete. The next step is to select all the emails in which you are copied. It's safe to assume that there is no direct action required from you in these emails, so you should be able to scan through them quickly, and delete or file as many as possible.

Again, don't fully read or respond to any emails yet.

Step 4. Now make a temporary folder called Inbox Holiday and drag all the remaining emails from your inbox into that folder. Remember that by the end of the day, this temporary folder needs to be deleted. Since all the emails you received during your holiday are now out of sight, you can start with a fresh, clean inbox, and apply the *15-Minute Inbox* principles to all your new emails straight away.

Step 5. Take 30 emails from your Inbox Holiday folder and drag them into your inbox. Use the 4+1 Action Ds (Delete, Deal, Defer, Delegate and Done? Next) and clean up this batch quickly. When you're ready, take the next 30 emails from your Inbox Holiday folder and do the same. Repeat this process until you've dealt with your whole backlog. Then delete the temporary folder.

More about exploded inboxes

Most inboxes that belong to an organization have a storage limit. 100 MB or 5 GB – whatever the number, there is a limit. When this limit is reached, new emails will not make it to your inbox. The sender will receive an automatic message that their email couldn't be delivered, and you won't even know about it.

But even before hitting the limit, your email program slows down; loading your inbox takes longer and longer, and you might be bombarded with warning messages about your full inbox.

When this happens, it is good to know which folders are consuming your limited storage so you can clean them up. Clearly, your inbox is one of the contenders, hence this book. Other folders that are impacting on your storage availability are "Sent" and "Trash." And to the surprise of a lot of my clients, your calendar is also consuming megabytes, especially when you store appointments with attachments.

Cleaning up folders is relatively easy – it could be that you just need to drag and drop emails into your personal folders. Since the way to clean up your calendar depends on your email program, you might want to consult the Help option or contact your IT help desk when you are facing the overloaded calendar issue.

Explosive dreams

You need to have your smart phone next to your bed to set your alarm, don't you? So why not have a quick look at your emails at the same time, just before you go to sleep? Well, actually, that's not a good idea.

When you look at your emails just before going to sleep, a few things happen that you need to know about. Firstly, you activate your mind and make it start thinking again, while what you really need for a good sleep is a rested mind. In addition to that, you also trigger subconscious brain activity – such as a reaction to a negative email – which prevents you from sleeping. Let's say you get an email late at night making some kind of complaint or comment about your work. What can you do about it immediately anyway? Nothing. So, what was the purpose of reading it? Emails like that emails can wait until your next working day.

If you are serious about focusing your time and attention on activities that really matter, checking your emails before you sleep is a habit to stop. Set your smart phone settings so your emails won't disturb you between 10pm and 7am, or even leave your phone or tablet in another room. Whatever method you use to improve your discipline, make sure you tackle this issue.

And if you are the manager who is sending email at times when your team members are enjoying their personal time, consider putting a delay on the delivery of your message, so it arrives the next morning. One of my clients who uses the delayed delivery approach actually deletes a lot of the emails he had drafted when he looks at them with fresh eyes, realizing they don't need to be sent at all.

Email disaster stories

One morning, I received this email from one of my coaching clients (names are changed, of course).

Needless to say no explanation is required as to why using email for this kind of communication is not a good idea.

> *From: Charlotte Lang*
> *To: Joost Wouters*
> *Subject: Urgent (I need help)*
>
> *Hi Joost,*
>
> *I made a TERRIBLE mistake today.*
>
> *My colleague Madeline has been with the company for a long time, but she has never been able to reach her targets (far from it). I would perhaps say that she's very 'square' in the way she works, that she is stubborn and unwilling to change things (the system always has to be changed to fit her, etc.).*
>
> *But that aside, my mistake was a FATAL one. I wanted to send an email to Robert (my sparring partner) to share my frustration, and I put it very bluntly in this email that "Madeline deserves the finger", that "it's her own fault if she doesn't reach her targets" and finally "how difficult can it be?" and by mistake (I was too quick) I sent this*

to HER – of ALL people!

She read it and replied: "Thanks for your email. I think that the tone is rather vulgar."

I immediately went to apologize but she had gone. So I sent her an email and I will go and see her tomorrow. I really wanted to apologize, of course. But the mistake's been made and I cannot unmake it.

This is terrible – any good advice on how I can/should solve/tackle it?

Thank you!
Charlotte

Here's how I replied:

Hi Charlotte,

Well, isn't this interesting?

I can imagine how terrible you feel, but take a deep breath and try to put a little smile on your face about such a silly mistake. :-)

The world will not explode, the sun will rise tomorrow (most probably) and you do need to apologize to her.

You can apologize for the fact that you "gossiped" about her and talked about her in a disempowering way to someone else. If you wanted to address this issue you should spoken to her about it directly, instead of going to Robert.

However – and here comes the interesting part – you were right in some ways, so you don't have to 'over apologize'. You can even use this opportunity to say that this is how you feel about her behavior, and suggest that you talk about it with her.

And that's a lesson learned indeed.

Go for it. You can do it.

Big hug, Joost.

Loaded email

Every now and then, a juicy story pops up about a loaded email that was sent by mistake to the wrong person or people, like the previous example. But email is often used to send loaded news on purpose. A couple of years ago, 400 employees from Radio Shack were fired via email. Not exactly the best medium for communicating serious news like this.

Last year, the management team of one of my clients was in a battle with the board of the Trade Union about the discontinuation of some work contracts. To show their disagreement, the Union emailed all employees sharing their point of view, including in the message the names of the three people whose contracts were due to be discontinued. These people didn't know before the email was sent that their jobs were in danger – you can imagine the upset this caused, not to mention all the time and energy that was wasted afterwards in discuss and explain the mistake.

The golden rule here is this: If your message is likely to shock someone or generate a negative emotional response, don't use email to deliver it.

The emotional weight of an email

One of the many misuses of email is using it to avoid direct confrontation. Of course working closely with other people – often under time pressure – can sometimes lead to conflict. And dealing with conflict is not something most of us look forward to. Lucky we have email, right?

He's done it again, and this time you're really upset. So you roll up your sleeves and spent a good half hour crafting an email that clarifies your position once and for all. You get to include your opinion about the topic, and attempt to resolve the conflict. You re-read it a couple of times to make sure you stated your case clearly and didn't offend the recipient too much, you copy your boss and then you hit Send.

Boom!

You might as well have thrown a hand grenade into his office – metaphorically speaking, the effect is more or less the same. An attack via email can be much more destructive than a direct confrontation. Maybe this is because the recipient is taken by surprise, or because the human aspect of interaction is disconnected by the email. Either way, the impact on the recipient of a challenging email can be much bigger than that of a direct one to one conversation, in which you can adjust your behavior and responses according to the recipient's reaction.

The few kilobytes that a confrontational email weighs carry an emotional weight that is much more significant. People can lose sleep over a confrontational email they received during the day; they end up having a negative effect on the recipient's life.

The E in email is for electronic, not emotional

During my first year running my consulting firm, I ran into a conflict with a colleague trainer about which one of us 'owned' a certain client. We'd had a successful start with our programs with this client, and I was very eager to grow our business with them in a consistent and professional way. In other words, I wanted to do it my way.

My colleague trainer, however, also had some contacts at the company, and was speaking with them separately. Since I wanted to protect 'my' client, and keep all our communication consistent (i.e. coming from me), we ended up having an argument. And because I felt so right about this, we didn't solve our conflict in just one discussion; it took several weeks.

155

Of course, it wasn't all just face-to-face – we also communicated our different points of view via email. I can remember feeling sick if I opened my inbox and saw a new email from her. Reading an email can trigger all sorts of emotions: anger, frustration, confusion, sadness, and fear (in this case of losing money).

Looking back on this situation, experiencing the emotional effect of email first hand made a real impression on me. This experience shows that you should never make the 'e' in email stand for 'emotional'. Email is the worst – I repeat, *the worst* – communication tool when you're feeling angry, upset, revengeful or frustrated. I am sure you have had experiences of your own that prove this point.

Don't waste your time and attention

The most important reason not to confront people by email is that in a tense situation, an email is more likely to add fuel to the fire than extinguish it. If someone who is angry or upset with you expresses this via email, it doesn't matter how hard you try to explain or defend yourself in your reply, they will read into it what they want to prove their point. If you really want to reply, a simple 'I'm sorry' – without any added explanation – is usually the only useful option.

Of course, the same logic goes for you too. When you feel upset or angry, don't express it in an email. Pass by your colleague's desk, call her, or just let the emotion settle (always advisable anyway), but don't use email to make your point. Be brave: face the 'enemy' in person and explain your feelings.

Unless, of course, you want to waste your precious time and attention crafting dangerous emails. That's the other reason not to email someone when you're angry with them: these email conversations are often extremely time consuming for both sides.

If you feel that someone has treated you unfairly, you react by rolling up your sleeves, sitting purposefully behind your computer and throwing your feelings and opinions into a blank new message window. It takes you some time to choose the right words; you read and re-read what you've written, edit and re-edit some sentences until you think you have made your point perfectly clear. Then you hit the Send button.

How much time have you just spent on this confrontational email? Half an hour? An hour? More?

Your email blasts into the recipient's inbox. She reads it and re-reads it, and your email makes her upset too. After taking an hour or so to recover from the shock, she rolls up her sleeves, sits purposefully behind her desk, and start throwing her feelings and opinions into the blank reply. It takes her some time to choose the right words; she reads and re-reads what she has written, edits and re-edits some sentences until she thinks she has made her point perfectly clear. Then she hits the Send button.

How much time has she just spent? Half an hour? An hour? More? And bang! Here it is in your inbox again. Tag – you're it.

Is it clear yet that email is not the right tool for solving conflict? We should never use email to express that we are angry or upset. Never. And we shouldn't allow it in our teams either.

One last point if you're not convinced: email has a long memory and messages are still traceable very far in the future. Emails that contain things you said about someone in the heat of the moment a year ago (and probably regret now) can pop up at the most inconvenient times. They might be rediscovered by the recipient, or – even worse – be forwarded to someone. And even if you think you have deleted a negative email, a copy will be safely stored on the main server just to keep you guessing.

157

How to deal with upsetting emails

You're probably not someone who writes confrontational emails when you're angry or upset (especially after reading all that...), but what do you do when you receive a message that pushes your buttons?

Albert Einstein once said, "We cannot solve problems at the same level at which we created them." This certainly applies to communication problems. A very important rule of thumb is to go one communication level up when an issue arises.

So if you receive an email that upsets you, you need to go one communication level up to solve it: phone the person. If that doesn't work, you can consider a one-to-one conversation (or video or web conference if the other party doesn't work in the same building). Direct conversation is the most powerful way of communicating: Nothing beats a conversation between two human beings.

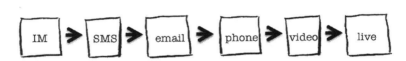

Before you go to the next level, always make sure you have cooled off. Breathe. Never reply, regardless the method of communication, when you are angry or upset. This will just make things worse. I am sure you have plenty of evidence in your own experience bank.

Step 4:

L is for Leverage and Liberation

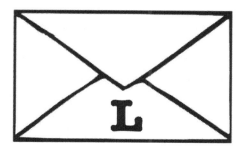

Free at last! With your newly acquired skills and habits, you can now create extra time every day. You can dedicate the time you used to spend on inefficient email management to your business instead. Or to something else that is important to you.

In this fourth M.A.I.L. step, you will explore how you can make your life even easier by leveraging the email concepts you have learned, and training the people in your team to master their inboxes too.

And the most important part of this step is creating a powerful plan to help you achieve the results you're really after in your life. I will introduce a proven successful planning methodology, which has helped me personally for over 12 years, enabling me to live my life the way I want to.

Spending time answering emails doesn't come into it!

CHAPTER SIXTEEN

Leverage Email Awareness

"If you think you are too small to be effective, you have never been in bed with a mosquito." – Betty Reese

The more, the merrier

The positive impact of *The 15-Minute Inbox* grows exponentially as more and more people begin to follow the steps. For every person in your contact list who applies the principles introduced in this book, you will notice an overall reduction in the flow of email traffic. This will make your life easier, as well as enabling your contacts to spend more time and attention on activities that really matter to them.

That's a real win-win situation.

In this chapter, we will explore what you can do to increase supportive email behavior in the people around you. It doesn't matter what your opportunity for leverage is. Whether you are leading the whole organization, a department, a team, or you are reporting to someone yourself; you can always positively influence your email environment.

Of course, the more people you can influence from your position, the more vital your contribution to changing the email environment.

Wake up!

I have never met a General Manager who would willingly accept a situation where everyone in their organization spends hours a day keeping themselves busy with internally focused, unproductive email ping-pong. And almost all of them are letting it happen. And they are usually part of the game themselves.

Why did you hire the people in your team? What is the biggest value a Marketing Manager can bring to the organization? What about the Finance Director? Or the Key Account Manager or a Demand Manager? What value do you bring to the organization?

The biggest asset of your employees and colleagues is the time and attention they can spend on marketing, financial, sales or supply challenges. They can make a difference in their fields, given the time and attention. That's why you pay them such good salaries.

In my work within different industries over the last 12 years, I have noticed that companies within an industry are becoming more and more similar. If you look for instance within the fast-moving consumer goods industry, a company like Procter & Gamble is the same as Unilever, is the same as Reckitt Benckiser, is the same as Johnson & Johnson, is the same as Colgate Palmolive.

I'm exaggerating of course, but to a large extent these companies are very similar: They focus on the same target audience, produce the same commodity products, compete in the same saturated markets and product categories, and even work with the same managers. Just look at some people's career paths on LinkedIn.

This similarity with in an industry means that you have little room to maneuver – you can make a difference with roughly 10 percent of your activities. Within this 10 percent, you need to make your approach distinct form the competition and gain market share points in a crowded environment.

Within this 10 percent, you just don't have the luxury of time to waste – your team can't waste their time and attention on un-necessary internal email activities. In the end, it costs you much more than the physical hours they waste: The biggest cost is in failing to tap into the huge potential you have available because they couldn't focus their time and attention on activities that would really move your organization ahead.

Grow your circle of influence

If you're not the CEO, it will be difficult to change the email cul-ture in your organization overnight. And even if you are, it won't be a simple task either, since the way your employees deal with email is likely to be deeply ingrained in their daily routines.

In his book *The Seven Habits of Highly Effective People*, Stephen Covey describes Circles of Concern and Influence. Your Circle of Concern includes the wide range of concerns you might have, including your health, your children, problems at work, the amount of government borrowing, or the threat of hyperinfla-tion. Your Circle of Influence encompasses those concerns that you can do something about. They are concerns that you have some control over.

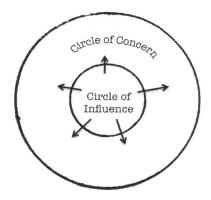

Covey defines 'proactive' as being responsible for your own life. Your behavior is a function of your decisions, not your conditions. Proactive people focus on issues within their circle of influence. They work on things they can do something about.

Your circle of influence with regards to a changing email environment starts with you, regardless of your function or position. From here on, you can slowly but surely grow your influence to encompass your team, department and organization.

Lead by example

Mahatma Gandhi once said, "Be the change that you wish to see in the world." The best, most effective way to inspire others to adjust their email behavior is to be the change you want to see in your team or organization.

It starts with a bold stand for your own time. It is your time and your attention. It is your life. Don't allow your agenda to be ruled by other people's emails.

From this stance, you probably need to break some email routines and behavior. And your colleagues will start to take notice of this. They'll receive fewer emails from you, and those that do arrive will have clearer calls to action. They might also receive a request to remove you from a distribution list, or a reply to a long, confusing email saying, "Please drop into my office, that will save us a lot of email ping-pong."

It is very likely that you'll need to inform or re-educate the people around you. A friend of ours became Managing Director of a public broadcasting company. He received hundreds of emails every day, mostly with him in copy, informing him of everything that was going on (or, in his words, "to show how hard they were working"). He quickly organized a meeting with his teams where he clearly stated his email rules:

"Only send me an email if I need to take a specific decision. The rest of the information I will hear during our meetings, where we can discuss any open issue."

Overnight, he reduced his flow of incoming emails to just 10 a day. When the occasional 'wrong' email entered his inbox, he replied simply with "What's the decision you're asking me to take?" By doing this, he set a clear example for communication to all his team leaders. This would also have had a big impact on the email behavior of everyone in the company.

It's not difficult to make a statement like this if you are in a leadership position. It just requires that you give up the need to be in control of everything – give up your micromanaging tendencies. By modeling good email practice, you can encourage the people around you to send emails only when it's necessary and appropriate.

Radically remove email inefficiencies

As we've seen, the more impact that you have based on your function, the more vital your contribution to changing the email environment. There are some inspiring examples in the market of leaders who found ways to improve email efficiencies.

Be on top of your own inbox first

Of course, this is what you're after – why would you be reading this book otherwise? But let's state it very clearly once more. You have to tackle the biggest email inefficiency first: you.

One of my clients had an average backlog of 2,000 emails. When he finally cleared and stayed on top of his inbox, both his email traffic and his meeting load went down. His colleagues finally got the direction and input they needed so they didn't need to hound him.

Make a powerful commitment

Some companies are taking drastic steps to help employees manage the number of emails they receive. The CEO of Atos, a French IT services company, has vowed to ban internal email[17]. Almost two years on, zero email has not only begun to take hold within Atos, but the initiative has attracted interest from a growing number of business leaders.

The question is, will these interventions and declarations solve the problem? As we have seen, email is often not the problem, just the symptom. But by making a bold statement like this, a leader can kick-start the awareness and discussions needed to tackle the root issues contributing to email inefficiency.

What statement can you make in your team about addressing the email overload issue? What rules can you install about the use of the Cc field to reduce the number of unnecessary emails you all receive?

Put a value on each email

One general manager I've worked with charges staff members

five Euros from their budget for each email she receives. Amazingly, her overload has gone down, the relevance of the emails she receives has gone up, and the senders are happy, too, because the added thought often results in them solving more problems on their own.

(I'm sure her finance manager doesn't calculate the exact budget implications at the end of the fiscal year, but it helps to leverage the awareness.)

Set email preferences

Like in the examples above, establish your email preferences: How often do you want to receive emails? When? About what? Make your preferences known throughout the company. When you're leading a project, don't default to being copied on everything. Indicate to your team when you should be copied on communications.

Likewise, ask your colleagues and staff for their preferences when it comes to you communicating with them. Do they feel overloaded?

Install other ways of communication

Emailing is a reflex. Need to share a file? Email. Need to ask a question? Email. Need feedback? Email.

Install five-minute meetings with your key team members every day where you discuss all relevant topics. Start each morning with your assistant and go through the day. Don't send an email if you need an urgent answer, but call instead. Install the ten-desk rule in your team: Within a zone of ten desks we will not send an email to each other. Or start Email Free Friday, just to experience the effectiveness of different ways of communicating.

What other methods of communication do you have available?

Avoid scattered information storage

Email can be an effective means for quick communication, but when it comes to collaborating with your team to get work done, it's a major hindrance to your team's productivity. Group conversations become unwieldy too quickly, and before you know it all of your team's important conversations and files are trapped in inboxes everywhere.

If you work in a team or on a project, make sure you install a central project platform, so you can keep track of the most current status updates and maintain clarity about what needs to get done, and by whom.

A positive side effect is that this way of working makes it much easier for new people to join the team and to transfer knowledge from one person to another.

Calibrate relevance

If you are constantly copied on emails despite requesting not to be, you could start replying to emails that aren't relevant with a single word: "Relevant?" Or "What is the decision you want me to take?" This will help your colleagues learn what is and isn't relevant to you.

It's important to explain to them beforehand that the goal is to calibrate relevance, not to criticize or put them down. And encourage them to send you relevancy challenges as well - perhaps you could improve your own calibration.

Train your team

The principles covered so far are perfectly suited for a quick team training session. You can involve HR if needed, and set up a training session. Or you can do it yourself in your team.

I have experienced that training everyone in a team at the same time has a huge effect on team productivity. When a participant once shared that she frequently spent an hour crafting the perfect email, with all the potentially relevant information included, only to hear from her colleagues that nobody was reading her emails because they were too long and detailed, something became very clear to her. Now she emails people succinctly, and calls them when it's more appropriate.

In another session, several managers were complaining to their director, who was also in the training session, about the level of detail he requested from them in emails. He was happy to clarify his needs and change his email behavior, helping to reduce everyone's email load.

What could the results be in your team? What opportunities will arise when you leverage the email awareness in your team? What role can you play in paying this awareness forward?

CHAPTER SEVENTEEN

Liberation: Where is Your Plane Going?

"If you don't know where you are going, you will probably end up somewhere else." – Lawrence J. Peter

Free at last

You've almost reached the end of the four M.A.I.L. steps – L is for Liberation. In my experience, this is the most powerful step – the one I'm most passionate about, and the one that had (and still has) the biggest positive impact on my life. Like Abraham Lincoln said, "the best way to predict the future is to create it."

The methodology I have used for creating my future over the last 12 years is called Best Year Yet®. This is a simple yet powerful process to make the best out of the 12 months ahead of you. Thanks to this process, I: made the step from Executive Team member at PepsiCo Benelux to owner of my Management Consultancy firm; grew our gross sales to $1 million in the third year of our business; traveled across the USA for a year in a '93 Ford Winnebago motorhome with my family; climbed Mont Blanc; moved to Spain and built my dream house in the Mediterranean; and met a lot of inspiring colleagues worldwide. How's that for results?

I'm going to take you through a key part of this planning process; you can delve into the whole concept by reading *Your Best Year Yet!* by Jinny Ditzler.

You can also register with the Best Year Yet System and create your liberation plan directly online. In addition to a guided step-by-step process to help you make your plan, you can access a powerful tool to track your plan over the coming twelve months, and receive expert information on becoming a master at producing results during the year to come. You can register for the Best Year Yet System at www.15MinuteInbox.com/BYY.

For now, you can complete the steps below to experience the process. You can always feed them into the Best Year Yet System later if you wish. I strongly recommend you write down your answers instead of doing this as a mental exercise, so make sure you have a pen or pencil and paper handy.

What does your life look like from 30,000 feet?

Let's forget your desk, your computer, and your inbox for a while. Let's step into a plane, take off and fly to an altitude of 30,000 feet. Now look at your life from this distance. Observe the different areas of your life. Can you see your office, your colleagues, your family, your kids' school, the restaurant where you like to eat with your partner, the houses where your friends live, the park where you like to run with your dog, the gym where you work out, the beach you like to visit at the weekend? Can you see all the areas of your life?

All these areas form part of the life you live right now. Maybe there are also areas that are not visible yet, like the trip you'd like to go on, the book you'd like to write, or the partner you hope to meet.

I always like to 'fly out' and have a look at my life from a broader perspective. Especially after periods of heavy working, when my life only seems to consist of projects, emails, meetings and long hours. Flying out puts everything back into perspective, and enables me to make an assessment of where I am and how I'm doing.

1. What do you like about your view?

If you look at all the areas in your life like the ones described above – and you can probably add many more – think about what works in your life. What are the things that you're happy about, that you're proud of, that you consider to be a success? These don't have to be huge accomplishments, like winning a marathon; they could be things that are significant to you, like having received a compliment from you manager yesterday, or closing an important sale, or even having participated in a marathon.

This is something that we, as human beings, are not very good at. We like to focus on things that go wrong, failures and negative news. If someone gives us a compliment, we quickly add "yes, but..." and if we open a newspaper or watch TV, we don't tend to get a lot of positivity either.

So, what do you *like* about your view? Scan through the different areas of your life and write down all the things that you enjoyed over the last year. Maybe you got the promotion you were after. Or you had a nice dinner with your partner. You delivered the sales figures as promised. Or you celebrated your kids' birthdays with the family. You visited your parents last weekend. Or you're still in good shape.

This exercise is for you; don't worry about anyone else reading it. Just start writing and don't censor yourself. You can use the space below, but if you need more, grab a piece of paper and keep writing. And it's ok to include personal and work related accomplishments.

What works in your life?

_____

_____

_____

_____

_____

_____

_____

2. What do you not like about your view?

I assume that when you look at the areas of your life from a distance of 30,000 feet, you can also see many areas you're less happy with. Projects that don't go as planned; relationships you're disappointed with; feelings of failure. So now it's time to repeat the previous exercise, but this time thinking about all the things that don't work in your life right now.

Although we're much better at focusing on the negative side of a situation, we tend to always put the blame on others. It's much easier to say things like "My boss didn't give me the promotion I deserved." Or, "They send me too many emails, my inbox is always overloaded." Or, "My partner has left me, and now I have to deal with the mess."

The challenge is to define disappointment in such a way that it describes your role in it, or how it affects you. So look out of the plane window at your life and write down all the things that you're not happy about. Maybe you feel overwhelmed by all the projects on your plate. Or you missed your daughter's birthday because of a business trip. Maybe you gained five kilos when you were trying to lose them. Or you don't spend enough time with your partner. Or when you're home with your family you're always checking your emails.

Again, this is your exercise so don't censor yourself. If you need more space, continue writing on a separate piece of paper. Good luck!

What doesn't work?

_____

_____

_____

_____

_____

_____

_____

3. What lessons have you learned so far?

Life is a collection of experiences. Some experiences feel good, others don't. If you look back over the two lists you just created, there is a lot of value in them in the form of lessons. What is the wisdom you already have in you that you see reflected in those lists? What are the things, behaviors and actions that work for you that you can identify in list number one, which you forgot or overruled in list number two?

Lessons that work for me when I look at my life from 30,000 feet are:

Go for a walk when angry.

Align my time and attention.

Complete before continuing the next project.

Celebrate successes.

Change point of view.

Listen to understand.

Now go through your two lists of accomplishments and disappointments and write down the three most important lessons that you can draw from them: The things that you know work for you, and that would make your life more sparkling if you applied them more often.

1 _____

2 _____

3 _____

4. Create a mindset that supports you

In the section Mirrors and Mindsets, we saw that in order to achieve the results you are after, you need to have a mindset that supports you. Your mindsets or paradigms can truly empower you. If you believe, for example, that you will always find a solution, you will probably look forward to facing the next challenge. However, if you have a paradigm about speaking in public that is not empowering you, a presentation in front of an audience will probably not make you very happy.

In order to create a mindset that will support you in achieving your best year yet, answer the following questions.

How do you limit yourself?

Here are some examples of how I limit myself:

I always present a solution immediately instead of listening first.

I get irritated when someone doesn't understand what I'm saying straight away.

I don't clean up my desk, kitchen or car.

I postpone doing administrative things that I need to do.

I start new projects without completing the previous ones.

You get the point? Now what about you? How and where do you limit yourself?

_____

_____

_____

_____

In what areas of your life do you not achieve the results you want?

_____

_____

_____

_____

What do you say to justify or explain these failures?

_____

_____

_____

_____

The answers to this last question are your limiting paradigms. And as you saw in Mirrors and Mindsets, a paradigm or mindset is a way to see reality. It is your truth about a specific person or situation. This means that you can create new 'truths' as new empowering paradigms that will support you in achieving your best year.

Have a look at your list of limiting paradigms, and pick out the one that would most likely be in the way of you having a great year if you were to keep believing it. Think of the one paradigm that's having the strongest negative impact on you now, at this stage of your life.

What empowering new paradigm could overcome that obstacle?

It doesn't necessarily need to be the exact opposite of the limiting paradigm, just a positive and powerful statement that tackles the non-supportive mindset and supports you.

Here are some examples of empowering paradigms that my clients and I have created over the years:

The world is my playground.

I master my finances.

I am perfectly human.

New results show up fast in my life.

I enjoy learning from others and succeed far more quickly with their support.

Money is abundant and flows in and out my life.

I have a lot to offer.

What is your new empowering paradigm?

_____

_____

5. What are your core values?

By identifying the most important values in your life, you get an idea about what is really driving you. As Jim Collins wrote in *Built to Last*, companies that have identified and stick to their core values, regardless of the situation, are more likely to be categorized as one of the great existing organizations. Their core values are integrated in everything the company does.

The same goes for your personal situation. You have values that are true for you, which you want to demonstrate in your life. If you don't live up to them, or if you neglect them, you will not perform the best you can. Or you'll get bored. You're likely to end up with even bigger problems.

So, what are your core values? What is really driving you?

_____

_____

_____

_____

_____

6. What are the most important areas in your life?

Good job! Now that you have created an empowering paradigm to support you in your journey, and have a clear picture about what is really driving you, it's time to start planning your year.

An effective way to plan your plane's journey is to look from the perspective of the different areas in your life, and the different roles you play in life. If you are clear about which areas are the most important, it's much easier to define how you would like them to be.

Areas that are important to me, and roles that I play in my life, include being a father, manager, husband, consultant, family member (brother, son, brother in law), writer, colleague, sportsman, financial planner, traveler, photographer, parent at school, and one that I call my own coach (the role that takes care of my health and my personal development).

So take a look at your life and identify the roles and areas that are most important to you. Also list areas that you want to include in your life, but are not yet part of it. Maybe you want to become a parent, or write a book, or start painting or singing. Try to compress the list to a maximum of eight by combining areas where possible (for instance, in my situation I have combined brother, son, and brother-in-law as Family Member).

And don't forget to add a role that encompasses taking care of yourself, like your own personal coach.

What are the roles and areas of your life that are most important to you?

1 _____

2 _____

3 _____

4 _____

5 _____

6 _____

7 _____

8 _____

7. What area needs your focus for the next 12 months?

Now that you have defined the eight most important areas and roles in your life, you're going to have a look at the current status by evaluating how satisfied you are with your performance in each area or role.

You see the wheel below with the eight slices? Each slice represents one of the areas you have identified and runs from zero at the center to 10 on the outside. Make a wheel like this and write the names of each area or role at the end of each slice.

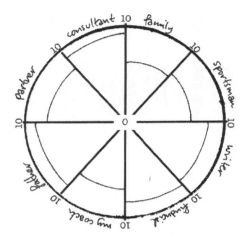

Give each area a score that represents how you rate your current performance in that area or role. Rate it 10 if you are completely happy and satisfied with your performance in that area. If you're 50 percent satisfied, put the score at five, and so on. If you do nothing in this area, or if you're very disappointed with your performance, leave it at zero.

Don't over-think each score too much; it's better to follow the first, spontaneous number that pops up. Draw a line in each slice that corresponds with the score (like in the example). You can color the area in if you want.

When you're ready, look at your wheel. Is it perfectly round? Does it have some bumps? It's not so much about the score of each area, but whether they are in balance, enabling the wheel to roll smoothly.

What area would you like to focus on over the next 12 months?

What is the one area that you know needs the most attention from you? That could have the biggest positive impact on your life if you addressed it. Or the biggest negative impact if you neglected it. This is your major focus for the coming year.

_____

_____

Your focus area can change over time. I remember that one year my major focus was being a successful entrepreneur – having just started my own business – and the year after my focus was on my relationship with my wife.

The major focus could be work related or a more personal role. In fact it doesn't matter. What you will see is that there is no real separation between your work and your personal world. One area has an effect on the other and vice versa. If you are success-ful in your role as manager, and you're going through a divorce, your role as a husband is affecting your role as a manager. The same applies in the positive: If you feel happy because you had a lot of fun in the car taking your kids to school, your colleagues in the office will notice.

8. Creating a successful future

What would things look like if everything was perfect in the ar-ea you want to focus on? Forget about the situation you're cur-rently in; instead, think about the future and visualize this area and your performance the way you really want them to be. What do you want this area – and your performance in it – to look like one year from now?

How would you describe it?

What do people say around you; customers, colleagues, your partner, your manager, your kids?

How do you feel?

What do you do, how do you behave?

What words describe it?

What colors illustrate it?

What music or songs would best fit this ideal situation?

Imagine it as a vivid full feature video playing in front of you. And if you have difficulties imagining it, write it down or make drawings on a piece of paper. Make the future very specific, but don't compare it to your current situation. What I mean by this is don't use phrases like 'it will be better' or 'we will have recuperated our market share'; just describe the situation as it is from a place one year from now, from a successful future.

Let's say you want to focus the next year on an area called 'Father' or 'Mother'. One year from now, in your ideal future, you come home from work and have dinner with your family, and everybody is sharing stories about their day. You tell your family a funny story about how you successfully dealt with a difficult client and everybody laughs. After dinner you all clear the table, you take your kids to bed and read their favorite book to them. You then sit with your partner on the couch and evaluate the day while sipping a warm cup of tea. Finally, you go to bed and... (you fill in the details).

Key words describing the perfect future of your major focus area:

_____

_____

_____

_____

_____

_____

How did you get there?

The next step will be to look back from this future and see how you got there. How did you get from where you were, one year ago, to this level of success you're enjoying?

The way to answer this question is to describe the specific results you achieved to reach your ideal future. In other words, what are the specific goals you have to define today that, once realized, will culminate in your ideal future one year from now?.

For the example above, specific and measurable results could be:

I take my kids to bed and read them a story three times a week.

I master my inbox and don't deal with emails when I'm at home.

I have taken a massage course with my partner.

I have read 10 new books.

Perhaps you pictured yourself in the future as 'being healthy'. However, without any additional details, it's too vague to really understand. What is considered healthy? Instead, some very detailed and descriptive goals could be:

I weigh ___ kg.

My body fat % is ___.

I am able to run ___ kilometers or miles.

I eat nutritious balanced meal at least five days a week.

I exercise three times a week.

Note that you should make your goals specific and measurable and describe them as results already achieved. Remember, you are looking back from the future. They should also be aligned – and definitely not in contradiction – with your core values. So, what are the specific results you have achieved in your major focus area one year from now?

1 _____

2 _____

3 _____

4 _____

5 _____

Of course, you can do this exercise for each of the eight areas you have described in step 6, and in the Best Year Yet System you will create specific goals for each role. For now though, I just want to stick with your major focus area.

9. Your liberation plan

The thing that I like best from this process is that you now have a plan that fits on one page.

```
My Plan

Guidelines
1. _____
2. _____
3. _____

New Paradigm


Major Focus


Top Results
1. _____
2. _____
3. _____
4. _____
5. _____
```

Copy the Guidelines you have created, your New Paradigm, your Major Focus, and the Top Results you want to achieve into your one-page plan. Now you have your own personal plan that you can look over with just a glance – enjoy it! (This is much better than those multipage business plans that collect dust in drawers or on shared drives.)

10. How do you make sure you make it happen?

This is probably the most important question in the process. And as we learnt in the section Implement and Integrate, if you don't get in motion, nothing will change. A structure to support you in achieving your goals is crucial. Here are some suggestions that have worked for me.

Make your plan visible: Print it and stick it in a place where you see it regularly, like your desk, office, or toilet.

Make your plan public: Inform the people around you about your intentions and goals. If you inform your kids about your goal to read to them three times a week, you have created a powerful support system. The same goes for the massage course with your partner. They will remind you!

Define small action steps: Every journey starts with the first step, and this one's no different. Don't try to change your life in one day, it won't happen. Instead, define small specific action points that will get you a step closer to achieving your goal. For example, 'Order three new books on Amazon,' or 'Bring back my email backlog to zero.'

What are the first action steps you can define to make your plan happen?

_____

_____

_____

_____

_____

Track your plan and adjust accordingly: Make sure you evaluate the progress of your plan at least once a month. Adjust the action steps you need to take to close the gap between where you are and the end goal.

A powerful tool to track your monthly progress is included in the Best Year Yet System. It is called PRO™ (Producing Results Online) and it allows you to score the performance of each goal, visualize the progress with graphs, define your action steps, and many more things. There's also an audio lesson every month that will help you to become a master at producing results.
If you're interested in the Best Year Yet System, you can make a start by visiting www.15MinuteInbox.com/BYY.

The importance of having a plan

Well done and congratulations on your plan! Although most companies have a business plan, most individuals don't. People might know what they don't want or don't like, but it is estimated that only about one percent of people have a clear picture of what they want to achieve. So you now belong to a very select group of people.

Knowing where you are right now and having a clear understanding of where you want to be is half the job. The remaining half is the journey to get to your ideal future. And therein lies the fun – striving towards a goal; having a purpose. The moment you achieve a goal, you need to set a new one. Because the moment you run out of goals, or lack purpose in your life, you will struggle to find the motivation to start the day.

This is a dynamic that you can clearly see in companies. About three months before the end of the fiscal year, an organization makes its business plan for the next year. A lot of presentations take place with management to get the numbers aligned with regional or global expectations. And then the plan becomes the Plan with a capital P. For about 10 months the whole organization uses this Plan as a guideline to make decisions, introduce new products, invent new ways to go to market and measure performance, as in 'we are at index 90 versus Plan.'

It is clear that the lack of a plan would lead to chaotic situations. (I mean, it's already chaotic and often not transparent with a plan, let alone without one.)

In the next chapter, we will examine further how you can make sure you make your plan happen. For now, take another look at your plan and enjoy your achievement.

CHAPTER EIGHTEEN

Get Out of Your Inbox, Step Into Your Business

"If a man is called a street sweeper, he should sweep streets even as Michelangelo painted, or Beethoven composed music, or Shakespeare wrote poetry. He should sweep streets so well that all the hosts of heaven and earth will pause to say, 'Here lived a great street sweeper who did his job well.'" – Martin Luther King, Jr.

Do more of what only you can do

One of the challenges that leaders have when they grow in job responsibility is figuring out what they need to stop doing and what they need to pick up in terms of how to spend their time and attention.

The question to ask yourself is: "What is it that only I can do?"

However, don't answer this question from a personal perspective. You might be great at marketing, because you've worked in that department your entire career to date. But now that you're the Marketing Director or General Manager, you shouldn't spend time on a specific label design, or the execution details of an in-store promotion.

Therefore, a better way to phrase this question is, "What functions can only I, as the [your role], perform?" Or, "What is it that only I can do, given the role that I'm in and all of the unique resources and opportunities that come with it?"

You may be the only manager who can meet with a top regulator or persuade a key customer to stay. You may be essential to recruiting senior staff. But you should hold back from taking on other responsibilities that don't come with your function, even if you excel at delivering on them.

The same applies to any other level in an organization. A complaint I hear quite often is that "Everybody around here seems to be a marketer", as in everybody shares their opinion when Marketing comes up with a new plan. Indeed, you may be solid in marketing, but if your company is stacked with good marketing people and you are responsible for Demand Planning, your highest and best use is probably in that area. Don't just focus on what you do or like to do best. Look around and see how you can be most useful.

Stay away from the operational stuff

Many managers also spend too much time on operational details, such as the best flight to take or the type of car to rent during their next business trip. You should delegate such tasks, if possible, to someone who can do this better. A participant in one of our workshops once told a story that she was making a lot of copies in the hallway, when her boss passed by and remarked that she didn't pay her to use the photocopier.

Again, there is nothing wrong with making copies. It's not an inferior job. But it might not be the task with which you add the most value in your current role.

And here comes the link to your inbox. How many emails in your inbox are related to operational tasks, or have nothing to do with the activities with which you add most value? How many emails are simply distracting you, taking your time and attention away from the things that only you can do?

Where can your role make an impact?

If you think about this question, your list of things that only you can do as [your role] is not necessarily very long, but the impact of the list items could be very high.

What is it that comes with your role that enables you to get things done that others can't? It could be any number of things, including:

- *Decision making authority*
- *Visibility and credibility*
- *Representation of the organization*
- *Participation in leadership conversations*
- *Access to key people*
- *Overview of all agendas*
- *Support for certain functions*
- *Ability to get things moving*
- *Budget allocation*

With characteristics like this, your list of the things that only you can do might include getting rid of obstacles for your team, securing resources, building alliances, setting goals or energizing others around a vision.

Don't include activities just because you can do them or are good at doing them. Focus on the things that will really leverage the unique opportunities of your role.

Here's an example of my time at PepsiCo. I had invited a potential new client – the VP of a large pizza chain – to our head quarters to discuss the switch from Coke to Pepsi. I also invited my General Manager to join the meeting. During the preparation he asked me, "What is it that only I can do?"

"Let me see – be the General Manager. When I'm making that final presentation and discussing the conditions for the change over, I need you to act as our General Manager. I need you to show your interest, that you're well informed and say that you'll make sure we deliver for them. I don't need you to work with me on the third draft of the proposal or run the numbers for the fifth time. We've got other people who can do that. I need you to show up as the General Manager because you're the only General Manager we've got."

Get out of your inbox

In the previous chapter, we saw that having a plan with a clear direction is about half the job. The remaining half is the journey, the process of achieving your goals.

What can you do to make your plan happen and actually achieve the results you're after? It certainly won't happen from behind your computer! You probably need to work on emails every now and then to involve others and get the input you need to run your business. But don't let your business be run by your inbox.

You have to get out of your inbox and step into your business – no matter what your business is.

Disconnect from the email drip

My friend Brandon Burchard says it perfectly. Your inbox is nothing but a convenient organizing system for other people's agendas. They store their issues and items in it by directing them to *yourname@yourcompany.com*. If you're not working in Customer Services – where it really is your job to check email constantly – or on a project with a tight deadline where direct input via email is necessary, you should not be working in your inbox more than twice or three times a day.

Really. If you check your emails more often than that it's like you are on a drip. Every five minutes an email drips in and sets you into action. Correction - that should be reaction. And just like hospital patients on real drips, you cannot expect big action if you're on an email drip.

In the section Actions and Automation, you learnt how to manage and control the flow of incoming emails. Now it's time to get out of your inbox and step into your business. You now have a plan to achieve.

Of course, you'll still need email for certain communications, but it will be on your terms, serving the progress of your projects and your priorities.

Only when you have time left, and have completed the items on your list, can you have a look at other people's agendas and what they need from you. You have to manage your own world before you step into their worlds.

Don't manage your team from behind your inbox

I have one client where email is 'accepted' as the main method of communication. At least, that's what it looks like from a distance. It doesn't matter what time of the day I visit the office, people are sitting behind their desks and more often than not the program open on their desktop is their email client.

Some of them are directors, responsible for over 300 people, others lead departments of 50 people or team of 10. A lot of communication is going on. And most of it happens via email.

Over the last few years, the volume of emails being exchanged has increased year on year. The Radicati Group reports[18] that in 2011, the typical corporate email user received 72 email messages per day. In 2015, this is expected to be 84 emails, which means a growth of 16 percent in four years. Doesn't seem a lot, does it? That's the problem.

I'm sure you're familiar with the how to cook a frog analogy (just for the analogy, I hasten to add, I can't speak from experience). If you boil the water first and put in the frog, it will jump out immediately because of the high temperature. But if you put the frog in a pot of cold water and gradually raise the temperature, the frog will get used to the water and not notice the slowly increasing temperature. Until it's too late.

Email is a communication tool. It is not the communication itself. Like the map on your GPS is not the reality outside, just a representation of it. You will miss crucial information if you rely on these tools alone. As a manager you need to walk around, talk to people offline. The most important things are not said in an email; you need to have good relationships with people in your team to learn about them.

And you need to jump out of the pot before it's too late.

Walk around instead

Of course, it's not always efficient to walk around, and email has the great benefit of enabling you to communicate at a time that fits your schedule best, while the recipient can read your email when it suits them best. But there are still plenty of occasions when you can avoid sending an email.

One of the solutions I like is the 'Ten Desk Rule', where you don't send an email to anyone sitting within 10 desks of you.

Another is the 'Daily Check-In' – a quick five-minute gathering around your desk with all your team members, where you discuss the day, its biggest challenges, and who will be doing what. Make sure you keep it short and to the point, with everyone standing, and ensure that it lasts a maximum of 10 minutes and happens every day, regardless of what might come up. By following this practice you can avoid a lot of email traffic because team members will be clear on what to do and where everyone is.

One of the marketing managers that I coach starts his day by visiting each desk of his 10 brand managers. By doing so, he realizes more than one objective: His team members know that if they have a question they can save it for the next morning, avoiding a lot of email traffic during the day. He finds out first hand what's going on, and is therefore much better connected to the business than he would be relying on information via email. And, most importantly, he creates a team of engaged people, with human interaction. People love to work for him!

Have a look at your email traffic and identify the people between whom the most traffic takes place. You can encourage them to use a different method of communication to exchange information, and eliminate a big chunk of your emails in the process.

@CTION: What could you do or introduce in your team to reduce the amount of email traffic? Do it!

Make time to think

One of the complaints I hear in many management teams is that they lack the time to think. I asked several General Managers "If you could change one thing about the behavior of your people, what would it be?" One of them answered:

"Less email writing and more doing! People can spend their whole day managing their inbox. One of the biggest assets of our company is management's time and it should not be wasted on doing 150 emails a day – most of which are not adding value."

The paradox here is that people claim that they don't have time to think or take time off to think, because they have so many emails and other things to do. However, this short-term behavior leads to more inefficient emails that aren't well thought through, giving everyone even less time to think. This is a common Catch 22 situation.

The solution is simple. You have to break routines here, because there will never be time for strategic thinking if you just wait for it. You have to take charge of the gaps in your calendar (which, as we know, will tend to fill up) and block time to think.

Live and work abroad for three months each year

The first year I made my Best Year Yet plan, I included the following goal:
"We want to live and work abroad for three months each year."

Now, how do you do that when you've just started your own business and you need to look for clients and income? There are several answers to this question.

Firstly, I knew that this was one of my top goals that would be of vital importance to me. Every time I came back from a trip or a holiday, I was full of new ideas and actions. I needed time to think about the future, come up with new ideas and make plans to execute them.

Secondly, I made my goals equally important. I made them all business goals, be they related to my work or my private life. So living abroad for three months was as important to me as earning the same amount of money with my new business as I did with Pepsi. By doing that I didn't have to prioritize my goals, as they were all important (that's why I had to limit myself to a handful of top priorities).

Thirdly, I selected three periods of one month that I blocked in my calendar. It worked out brilliantly, because when one client asked me to meet them in mid February, I could say that I was not available then, but that I could see them in early March.

Finally, to make sure I would really go, I booked the tickets in advance, and also set up a routine whereby I would book the tickets for the next trip before I took off for the current one.

This goal has worked out for me brilliantly and has evolved over time. The year after my initial goal, we changed it into a round the world trip, two years later it became traveling around the USA in a motor home for a year, and finally, we ended up moving to Spain.

Recharge your thinking

How much time do you need in your current role each week to think without distractions or interruptions? To focus your full time and attention on the challenges you are facing. Half an hour? An hour? Half a day?

What time works best for you – not according to your agenda, but when you are most creative? And where could you concentrate best? Your office (probably not), your home (maybe), outside (probably)? You could, for instance, start each Friday morning with an individual offsite meeting. Block it into your agenda, find a cafe close by, and start each Friday from now on with one or two hours of strategic thinking. Enjoy a fresh cappuccino at the same time.

One of the most impactful decisions that Bill Gates took when working at Microsoft was to have 'Think Week' once or twice a year. Family, friends, and Microsoft employees were banned from his retreat. He was alone, in a nice location without distractions, with one or two predefined themes he wanted to tackle. And he's not the only one – Mark Zuckerberg and Steve Jobs took regular 'think weeks' to invigorate their thinking.

Spending undisturbed time off-site is one of the easiest and cheapest activities you can do that has enormous returns. And yet it seems so impossible... Well, if you keep holding on to that belief I sincerely hope you enjoy being a firefighter.

@CTION: Imagine a strategic thinking structure that works for you and block it in your calendar.

Taking time out for undisturbed strategic thinking isn't just something that benefits individuals. In my work with management teams I strongly recommend they plan two-day off-site meeting once every quarter. This meeting is not to discuss daily operations, but to examine the topics that really have an impact on the long-term health of the organization they lead. They could conduct a comprehensive strategy review, a review of their own teams' performance, a personnel review, or a competitive and industry review whilst enjoying a full day or two working together as a leadership team.

@CTION: Discuss this concept with your team and agree on a frequency at which you will sit together to recharge your strategic thinking as a team.

Protect your concentration

Almost all organizations that I currently work with have some kind of open office structure in place. This concept has great benefits, since it stimulates teamwork and helps communication between team members. However, one of the downsides is that the increased collaboration can reduce your concentration.

This means you have to find ways to protect your concentration, even when there are a lot of interesting stimuli around you to distract you from your work.

Buy comfortable headphones

The first thing to do to protect your concentration is to get yourself comfortable headphones. You can either use them to reduce external noise, or to put on some music to help you concentrate. Either way, you create your own bubble in which it is great to work. An added benefit is that other people can easily see that you're working and can't be disturbed. And even if not everyone reads the sign, you will definitely avert some interruptions.

Use the open door policy correctly

A lot of managers who have a door in their office believe they always have to keep it open as a sign of being an approachable manager. But apart from setting the wrong example by doing that, they also ruin their own concentration, because people will walk in and out throughout the day. The original 'open door policy' meant: If the door is closed, I'm at work; when it's open, feel free to enter.

@CTION: *If you have a door, use it correctly. And if you need to re-educate your team members, do it.*

Make use of fishbowls

Most open plan offices have silent rooms or small meeting rooms available. At P&G we had small glass offices, which we called fishbowls. Use them, either if you need silence to work on something, or if this helps to protect the concentration of others when you have to make a phone call or have a conversation with someone.

Effective meetings avoid a lot of email

Well-handled emails reduce meetings. And well-handled meetings reduce emails. Meetings are one of the most important tools for aligning an organization and creating the clarity needed to have all people working on the same priorities. Unfortunately they don't always work like that.

There are two problems with meetings, as described by Patrick Lencioni in his book *Death by Meeting*:

1. They are boring, tedious, not engaging, and dry.
2. They are ineffective; they don't contribute to the success of the organization.

Meetings are ineffective because they lack contextual structure. Most teams have one kind of regular meeting, with randomly focused discussions about everything from strategy to tactics, from *administrativia* to culture. Because there is no clarity around what topics are appropriate, there is no clear context for the various discussions that take place. In the end, little is decided because the participants have a hard time figuring out whether they are supposed to be debating, voting, brainstorming, weighing in, or just listening.

As a result, instead of creating clarity, a lot of meetings can add to the confusion – at least to the confusion about what is really important, or what has really been decided. And confusion inevitably leads to more emails with a more people in the Cc field, in an attempt to clarify the situation, whilst actually compounding it.

To make meetings more effective, you need to have different types of meetings, and clearly distinguish between their purposes, formats, and timings. Make sure you at least make a distinction between operational and strategic meetings.

The operational type of meeting is more tactical: you discuss the actual short-term issues. It will probably take place weekly and last about an hour to an hour and a half. Team members don't have to prepare much, because the topics are probably at the top of their minds.

The strategic type of meeting is more interesting and important. Here you and your team wrestle, debate, analyze, and decide on critical issues that will affect the organization in fundamental ways. It can last two to three hours, and you might discuss one to three topics. It requires preparation by all participants.

@CTION: Look at your current meeting structure and decide what clarity you can create in order to avoid a lot of emails during the time between meetings. Can you separate tactical meetings from strategic ones? If so, do it.

Meeting rules

Improve your meeting efficiency. If you plan to sit together with a group of people, make sure that everybody dedicates their time and attention to the meeting. Don't allow smart phones at hand or laptops open if there is no need for it. If people feel they can't contribute to a meeting, they should not be there at all. Tell them this, and be very clear about it. If they should be there, make sure they contribute. Don't allow anything else if you are leading the meeting.

And finally, if you are in charge of a meeting, make sure it starts and ends at the agreed time. It sounds obvious, but starting exactly at the announced time, even if not everybody is in yet, gives you a lot of power. It shows respect for the time and attention of the people who arrived on time, and sets an example for a constructive way of working together.

You can deal with these two topics by agreeing on meeting rules with your team. "What do we need to do to make our meetings more effective?"

Here are some examples from teams I've worked with:

No laptops or phones during meeting.

Only laptop use when needed for discussing the current topic.

Our meetings start and end on time.

If you attend, contribute.

Silence equals disagreement.

What could work for you?

_____

_____

_____

The ultimate time management system

You can save yourself two to four hours a day with the following system. It requires only five minutes of planning per day, and you need a week to 10 days to implement it correctly. The only thing it requires of you is discipline to stick with it. You have to do it every day, almost religiously.

Interested? Here we go.

Step 1. Decide when you will do your five minutes of planning. This can be either first thing in the morning or last thing the evening before, when you finish your day at the office. For some people the second option works brilliantly, because ideas pop up during the night; for others it doesn't work for that same reason.

Step 2. Make a list of the six most important tasks to accomplish that day. No more, no less. Take a piece of paper and on the top half you write them down as tasks with the result you want to achieve. This is not a to-do list; don't write "Artwork", but instead write "Artwork new labels approved."

Step 3. Write your estimation of how long the task will take. Make your estimates in 15-minute intervals and write them next to each task. You are in charge, so see what you can do to minimize the time needed per task.

Here's the key thing: You're planning for an eight-hour day. Not more. You have a maximum of six hours for your six tasks. If you need more, spread them into smaller tasks over the next few days, and write down results of each sub-task that you can do within your allocated time. Don't forget, you'll need about two hours for reactive work, including processing your emails. That makes eight hours.

Step 4. Plan your day. On the bottom half of the paper, draw a simple calendar. Number the tasks 1 to 6, and place them in the time slots. Don't forget to add the time slots for reactive work as well. You can of course also use the calendar function on your computer.

Plan the most confronting or difficult task as the first thing you do; when that is done, the rest of the day is easy.

Plan reactive work (email, phone calls) either before lunch or at the end of the day. You should never take them on first thing in the morning.

Don't add new things to your list if they pop-up – move them to your list for the next day.

This system is very powerful. It forces you to change some of your habits. And as you can imagine, it works if you work it. Plan your days only for six hours' work and make sure you put the tasks in your calendar. Don't forget to celebrate when you get your tasks done in those six hours. Treat yourself well.

And walk around in the time you have gained with this approach. Step into your business.

EPILOGUE

End of Message [EOM]

"You can't stop the waves, but you can learn how to surf."
– Jon Kabat-Zinn

Email

Years ago it was an event when you received one; nowadays, it's one of the biggest obstacles for productivity.

Email.

We love it and we hate it. Email is a fantastic communication tool if you use it correctly, and the biggest energy drainer if your inbox is overloaded.

But those days are over. I sincerely hope *The 15-Minute Inbox* has inspired you to get into gear and become a master of your inbox. To apply the behavior that's needed to manage your inbox in less than 15 minutes a day. And, most importantly, I hope you've generated some great ideas about what you want to spend your time and attention on.

And remember, it is your time and your attention. It is your life.

Welcome to *The 15-Minute Inbox* community.

Sources

Of course, many books, articles, stories and quotes have inspired me when writing *The 15-Minute Inbox*. Here is a list of links that will take you to my sources. If I have forgotten to mention one, please accept my apologies and let me know, so I can immediately correct it.

Notes:

[1&2]From PEWinternet.org

[3]psychology.about.com/od/cognitivepsychology/a/costs-of-multitasking.htm

[4]Isaac Newton (1642 - 1727)

[5]forbes.com/sites/carolkinseygoman/2011/04/26/the-myth-of-multitasking/

[6]ics.uci.edu/~gmark/chi08-mark.pdf

[7]mckinsey.com/insights/organization/recovering_from_information_overload

[8]news.stanford.edu/news/2009/august24/multitask-research-study-082409.html

[9]self-improvement-mentor.com/how-to-break-a-habit.html

[10]From *Brilliant Email* by Monica Seeley

[11]macworld.com/article/1139510/empty_your_inbox.html

[12]*Email metrics report*, MAAWG, Nov 2010

[13]wikipedia.org/wiki/Megabit

[14]self-improvement-mentor.com/what-is-a-habit.html

[15]self-improvement-mentor.com/habit-formation.html

[16]Lally, P., et al., *How are habits formed* (European Journal of Social Psychology 2010)

[17]Paul Taylor, *Atos' 'zero email initiative' succeeding* (FT.com)

[18]From Radicati.com

Websites:

15MinuteInbox.com
InboxZero.com

BrandonBurchard.com
BestYearYet.com
LifeHacker.com
BusinessBootCamp.com

Articles and videos:
choosehelp.com/internet-addiction/email-addiction-an-impulsive-compulsive-disorder.html
youtube.com/watch?v=z9UjeTMb3Yk
hbr.org/2011/05/managing-yourself-extreme-productivity/ar/1
inc.com/amy-buckner-chowdhry/reduce-email-overload-easy-ways.html

Books:
The Seven Habits of Highly Effective People by Stephen Covey
Getting Things Done by David Allen
Your Best Year Yet! by Jinny Ditzler
Built to Last by Jim Collins
Lifehacker by Adam Pash
Inbox Detox by Marsha Egan
Bit Literacy by Mark Hurst
The Four-Hour Workweek by Timothy Ferriss
Death by Meeting by Patrick Lencioni

Legal note

The 15-Minute Inbox®, Inbox 0®, Best Year Yet®, Inbox Zero®, Getting Things Done® and all other brand names mentioned in this book are registered trademarks of their respective holders.

More resources

As mentioned in Chapter Seventeen, a powerful resource for generating the results you are after is the Best Year Yet System.

In addition to guidance on making your personal development plan, you can also access an online tool to help you track your plan over the next 12 months, and receive expert information on becoming a master at producing results during the year to come.

You can register for this system at www.15MinuteInbox.com/BYY.

* * * * *

As a member of *The 15-Minute Inbox* community, you also have exclusive access to a unique tool I've created to support you in implementing your new email habits: The 30-Day Reminder Service. Sign up for free, and for the next 30 days you'll receive a daily reminder with a useful tip to keep you in line. (And yes, you will receive this reminder via email.) Go to www.15MinuteInbox.com/30Days, to get started immediately.

* * * * *

For downloads of useful documents, such as the "4+1 Action Ds Flowchart" or the "Play The Game Sheet", visit www.15MinuteInbox.com/Downloads.

About the author

Joost is a consultant, speaker and author. The world's top companies invite him to their offices for his expertise on building cohesive leadership teams and creating crystal clear plans.

"From an Executive Team member of one of the world's largest organizations to the owner of my own life. After implementing my own Best Year Yet plans, my life is a fully integrated one; doing the things that I want, integrating business, family, private and leisure time:

- Being the full-time father of my two sons, Ruben and Jonas
- Starting and building a successful management consulting firm with my wife, Frieda
- Attracting clients such as Unilever, Heineken, Sara Lee, Royal Dutch Telecom, Nestlé, Procter & Gamble, Imperial Tobacco, Vodafone, LG, Philips, ZARA and Reckitt Benckiser
- Traveling to Russia, South Africa, USA, Europe and South America for projects
- Generating an annual gross income of $1 million within three years of being in business
- Successfully climbing Mont Blanc as expedition member
- Writing a book and being a professional speaker
- Living and working abroad for three months each year
- Traveling across the USA in a motor home with my family for a year
- Adopting a new lifestyle with eating raw, living food only
- Moving to Spain, learning Spanish and starting a new life there
- Building a house and training location on a Mediterranean beach
- Finding the education for my kids that I wished existed when I was young

"All time is my time. There's no difference between work, private and leisure time. They're all part of the same thing at the same time. They're all seamlessly combined in one life. Oh yes, and my inbox is empty at least once every day.

"Impossible? An illusion? Naïve? A dream?

"That's what I (and many others) thought 12 years ago when I decided to quit my job as a member of the Executive Team of Pepsi Cola Benelux. But I realized that if I wanted to have a different life, I had to think, say and actually believe new thoughts.

"I started by changing my mindsets and perspectives in different situations. I then took the actions that resulted in the above list: in achieving my goals. I created my life and have made it the way I wanted it – this year, next year, every year. And, of course, I've experienced John Lennon's song too: Life is what happens to you while you're busy making other plans."

About Actimpact Consulting Team

We support General Managers and their leadership teams to overcome the obstacles against sustainable growth, and to be examples of the changes they want to see in their organizations.

Over the years we have seen too many Leadership Teams acting like reactive fire fighters rather than proactive business builders. We believe that most teams are wasting their leadership potential and the talents they have. When people get to the point where they start leading an organization, they can accomplish so much more. Your team just has to fulfill its leadership potential, because your organization looks to you and follows your example.

Over the last 12 years, we have worked with many multinational clients, such as Unilever, Heineken, Reckitt Benckiser, LG, Philips, Imperial Tobacco, KPN, Delta Lloyd, Allied Domecq, Campina, Uniekaas, Vodafone, Sara Lee, P&G, ZARA, and Nestlé in Europe, South Africa, Russia, USA and South America.

Actimpact Consulting Team has its headquarters in Spain, in an office with a beautiful view of the Mediterranean.

Note for HR managers and trainers

If you are interested in adding this book to your training portfolio, feel free to do so.

Experience shows that a combination of theory and practice works best in obtaining impressive and lasting inbox results with managers in any organization. Therefore, *The 15-Minute Inbox* concept described in this book perfectly fits in any company training environment.

Please respect the concept and sources, and include one book for each training participant. You can also purchase a copy of *The 15-Minute Inbox Training Manual*, which will help you facilitate this powerful course.

Send an email to *Training@15MinuteInbox.com*, and I will happily give you more information.

Looking for an inspiring speaker?

"Energetic and vibrant! With his positive attitude, incredible communication skills and profound business knowledge, Joost manages to establish a fruitful connection with us, the audience."

For more information about a booking, send an email to *Speaker@15MinuteInbox.com*, or go to www.SpeakersAcademy.com.

Thanks for your review on Amazon

As a last point, I'd like to ask you for a favor. If you found something of interest in *The 15-Minute Inbox*, I would really appreciate it if you could leave a review on Amazon (or the store where you purchased this book).

The positive impact of *The 15-Minute Inbox* grows exponentially as more people work according to the principles discussed in this book. I think a lot of people will benefit from being able to deal with their email overload, and maybe this will result in even fewer emails in your inbox!

Final note

As today's leading communication tool, email may be heading for the same destination as the fax. My kids hardly ever use email now, as Facebook, Whatsapp, Twitter, iMessage, and many others are much better equipped for quick daily conversations. However, for the time being email will remain the main communication tool in any office environment, due to the lack of a better alternative. Until that time you have no choice but to master this tool.

And you *can* do it! You can control your email and manage it in 15 minutes a day. You can create additional time by cutting away the waste of non-supportive email behavior. And you can spend your extra time on activities that really matter.

I have done it, many others have done it and you can do it. To be in control of your inbox and all the information that is flowing towards you day after day is worth every single minute you invest in getting there.

Remember, it is your time and your attention. It's your life. Good luck on your journey!

Joost Wouters

"You have brains in your head.
You have feet in your shoes.
You can steer yourself in any direction you choose.
You're on your own.
And you know what you know.
You are the one who'll decide where to go"

-Dr. Seuss

[EOM]

30934635R00126

Made in the USA
Lexington, KY
23 March 2014